How to Lead It: Primary English

Other titles from Bloomsbury Education

How to Lead It: Primary Science by Kirsty Simkin
How to Lead It: Primary Maths by Shannen Doherty
How to Lead It: Primary History by Alex Pethick
How to Lead It: Primary Geography by Emma Lennard
The Curriculum Compendium by Rae Snape
What Every Teacher Needs to Know by Jade Pearce

How to Lead It: Primary English

Tricia Moss and Sallie Stanton
Series editor: Jon Hutchinson

BLOOMSBURY EDUCATION
LONDON OXFORD NEW YORK NEW DELHI SYDNEY

BLOOMSBURY EDUCATION
Bloomsbury Publishing Plc
50 Bedford Square, London WC1B 3DP, UK
Bloomsbury Publishing Ireland Limited
29 Earlsfort Terrace, Dublin 2, D02 AY28, Ireland

BLOOMSBURY, BLOOMSBURY EDUCATION and the Diana logo are trademarks of
Bloomsbury Publishing Plc

First published in Great Britain, 2025 by Bloomsbury Publishing Plc
This edition published in Great Britain, 2025 by Bloomsbury Publishing Plc

Text copyright © Tricia Moss and Sallie Stanton, 2025

Tricia Moss and Sallie Stanton have asserted their rights under the Copyright, Designs
and Patents Act, 1988, to be identified as Authors of this work

Bloomsbury Publishing Plc does not have any control over, or responsibility for, any
third-party websites referred to or in this book. All internet addresses given in this
book were correct at the time of going to press. The author and publisher regret any
inconvenience caused if addresses have changed or sites have ceased to exist, but can
accept no responsibility for any such changes

Figure 5.1 © Rosa Jay / Shutterstock.com
Quotes from Ofsted documents and the Department for Education used in this
publication are approved under an Open Government Licence: https://www.
nationalarchives.gov.uk/doc/open-governmentlicence/version/3/

All rights reserved. No part of this publication may be: i) reproduced or transmitted in
any form, electronic or mechanical, including photocopying, recording or by means of
any information storage or retrieval system without prior permission in writing from
the publishers; or ii) used or reproduced in any way for the training, development or
operation of artificial intelligence (AI) technologies, including generative AI technologies.
The rights holders expressly reserve this publication from the text and data mining
exception as per Article 4(3) of the Digital Single Market Directive
(EU) 2019/790

A catalogue record for this book is available from the British Library

ISBN: PB: 978-1-8019-9650-1; ePDF: 978-1-8019-9651-8; ePub: 978-1-8019-9653-2

2 4 6 8 10 9 7 5 3 1 (paperback)

Cover design by Sophie Gordon

Typeset by Newgen Knowledge Works Pvt. Ltd., Chennai, India
Printed and bound in the UK by CPI Group Ltd, CR0 4YY

To find out more about our authors and books visit www.bloomsbury.com
and sign up for our newsletters

For product safety related questions contact productsafety@bloomsbury.com

Contents

1. **Leading English** 1

2. **Getting the best from research evidence** 13

3. **Progression in English** 29

4. **Curriculum design** 37

5. **Assessment** 55

6. **Teaching early reading** 73

7. **Beyond early reading** 93

8. **Writing** 115

9. **Handwriting** 139

10. **Spelling** 149

11. **Purposeful oracy** 163

12. **Monitoring and quality assurance** 183

13. **Implementing change** 203

Bibliography 219
Index 229

1 Leading English

> The job of English subject leader is, in our view, a wonderful one. It is an incredibly important role that offers the thoughtful teacher something to really get their teeth into. It offers intellectual and leadership challenge, and should be highly valued as much more than administration, co-ordination and collation of useful resources.
>
> Subject leadership offers you the chance to act as a custodian for a crucial subject – someone who leads on articulating the vision for English, and is engaged in research regarding curriculum content and associated pedagogy. It gives you the capacity to develop teachers across the school so they can teach the subject with confidence.
>
> We hope you will find this book a useful resource in undertaking this exciting challenge!
>
> In this chapter, we will cover:
>
> - the importance of English as a subject, both within the curriculum and for pupils
> - the complexity of English, and what this means for you as subject leader
> - exploration of the subject leader's role, including the 'persistent problems' framework for leadership, and what this means for English subject leaders
> - ways to develop your expertise
> - guidance on getting the most from this book.

Why English matters

English is a uniquely important and wonderfully complex school subject, with many interrelated strands. In English lessons, we ask pupils to think *about* the language they use, as well as to develop how they think *with* it. Throughout their time in school, pupils study a broad range of fiction and non-fiction texts in this language, and will be taught to respond through the same medium. Learning in English is highly symbiotic – for example, whilst learning the alphabetic code is key to reading, it also enables pupils to spell with accuracy; whilst reading literature is of value in its own right, it also provides pupils with models of excellence for their own writing.

Development in English is considered to be one of the most important aspects of the primary curriculum because of its wider value to children and society. The key components, which can be simplified as speaking, listening, reading and writing, are not only objects of study in their own right, but also ways to access the wider school curriculum (DfE, 2013). Pupil success at GCSE, including in science and maths, correlates significantly with reading ability (GL Assessment, 2020). The impact of literacy levels also extends beyond school, as they are related to adults' employment prospects, wellbeing and even life expectancy (Terevainen-Goff et al., 2022).

To deny a pupil competence in English is to deny them much more besides – and, therefore, the English subject leader has an important job to do.

More than a set of functional skills

Language is essential to human society, and literature explores the human condition. As such, the subject offers an unrivalled contribution to both the individual and humanity. This means that teaching and leading English isn't just an *important* endeavour: reading great books and poems; sharing children's responses, both deeply emotional and clearly rational; delighting in language and seeing pupils use it with increasing precision and creativity to communicate their exact feelings and thoughts – this is *joyful* and *gratifying* work.

As a school subject, English is related to the disciplines of linguistics and English literature, which, in themselves, are broad fields of study with many branches. The knowledge pupils encounter in the primary classroom is their induction to these fields.

When we gently guide pupils to understand that texts are intentionally constructed, we are introducing the idea that they can, therefore, be studied, analysed, interpreted and produced. When our pupils participate in lively prediction of what might happen next in their class reader, we are doing more than creating engagement. We are shining a light on narrative structure, illuminating how writers share or withhold certain information deliberately to plant seeds or create tension. We are revealing how techniques such as foreshadowing are used to drive narrative. When we consider grammatical constructions within a text, we are exploring some of the building blocks of tone and style. When we invite pupils to discuss and debate their ideas in response to a text, we introduce them to literary study, whereby meaning is developed and explored in relation to the views of others.

A complex domain

As we have seen, the aims of the English curriculum are broad. They are also contested and hard to pin down (Ashbee, 2021): in contrast to some other areas of the school curriculum, there is no clearly agreed body of knowledge that constitutes the English curriculum (Didau, 2021). The English programmes of study set out what pupils should be able to do – but, aside from vocabulary, spelling and grammar, don't specify what knowledge pupils need in order to build these competencies.

The danger of this is that, without strong and careful leadership, our sense of what English is can be dominated by statutory assessment requirements. Reading lessons can become little more than repetitive comprehension practice and writing lessons reduced to formulaic approaches to getting through the Teacher Assessment Frameworks (TAFs).

To guard against this, rather than being overwhelmed by this complexity, we encourage the English lead to lean into it. Remember, you are in the same boat as primary subject leaders across the country. Engage with different views, think carefully and, over time, build a vision for the subject within the context of your school. By taking a curious and interested approach to developing subject expertise, you will likely feel more confident in the decisions you make and your ability to lead.

The role of a primary English leader

The key roles of the effective subject leader can be summarised as:

- sharing the vision for English as a subject, actively advocating for its value within the curriculum
- collaborating with other teachers to share, refine and review this vision
- considering what should be included in the English curriculum

- liaising with others, for example your school's Special Educational Needs Coordinator (SENCo) and other subject leads, to work towards ensuring a coherent, accessible curriculum
- sharing and overseeing production of long and medium-term plans for English
- curating, reviewing and sharing high-quality teaching resources that align with your curricular goals
- promoting and embedding high-quality teaching of the subject, using the professional development of colleagues as a powerful lever for achieving this
- quality-assuring English teaching across the school, providing developmental feedback to teachers and senior leaders.

School leadership can be seen as an ongoing attempt to overcome barriers or problems in order to make improvements. These include persistent problems: ones that are universal – in that all schools experience them – yet are issues we can impact upon positively through an effective response (Kennedy, 2016). Barker and Rees advise that understanding the persistent problems school leaders face, and drawing on expertise to solve them within the context in which you work, is a helpful way to approach this aim (Barker & Rees, 2020).

Barker and Rees identify seven persistent problems of school leadership, which are outlined in the following table reproduced from the chapter 'Developing School Leadership', in *The ResearchEd Guide to Leadership*, 2020. We have included two additional columns, specifying how these issues might apply to English subject leaders and signposting which chapters of this book can help you develop in these areas.

AREA	PERSISTENT PROBLEM	MANIFESTATION FOR ENGLISH SUBJECT LEADERS	RELEVANT CHAPTER(S)
School culture	Establishing a professional and supportive school culture and enlisting staff contribution	• Articulating the vision for English to colleagues • Consulting with teachers on curriculum content and associated pedagogy • Being open to feedback and seeking to solve problems with colleagues through ongoing dialogue	• Chapter 3: Progression in English • Chapter 4: Curriculum design • Chapters 6–11, which cover reading, writing and oracy • Chapter 12: Monitoring and quality assurance
Development	Ensuring effective approaches to professional learning and development	• Creating a curriculum for professional development (PD) that focuses on what teachers need to know to deliver your English curriculum effectively • Designing and delivering and/or identifying and promoting subject-specific professional development	• Most chapters, each of which features professional-development ideas and plans related to its content • Chapters 6–10, on discrete aspects of the curriculum
Curriculum	Organising and teaching the curriculum	• Identifying and sequencing the content knowledge to be taught • Leading on the provision of effective implementation and enactment of the curriculum through quality resourcing and subject pedagogy	• Chapter 3: Progression in English • Chapter 4: Curriculum design • Chapters 6–10, on discrete aspects of the English curriculum

AREA	PERSISTENT PROBLEM	MANIFESTATION FOR ENGLISH SUBJECT LEADERS	RELEVANT CHAPTER(S)
Behaviour	Attending to pupil behaviour and wider circumstances	• Creating a shared understanding of the learning behaviours needed of pupils and working with colleagues to develop these in classrooms • Supporting staff to overcome the barriers to learning faced by pupils within English, including keep-up and catch-up strategies	• Chapters 6–10, on discrete aspects of the English curriculum

School improvement	Analysing and diagnosing problems; planning and implementing strategies for continuous educational improvement	• Developing and implementing effective quality-assurance processes that will enable you to:
		  • track what pupils know and can do against the curriculum intent
		  • identify the development needs of teachers in order to identify and implement an effective response
			• Chapter 11: Monitoring and quality assurance
			• Chapter 13: Implementing change

Administration	Managing an efficient and effective organisation	• Ensuring the availability of quality resourcing and ways of working that consider staff workload and promote efficiency and effectiveness	All chapters

AREA	PERSISTENT PROBLEM	MANIFESTATION FOR ENGLISH SUBJECT LEADERS	RELEVANT CHAPTER(S)
Self	Developing personal expertise, self-efficacy and self-regulation	• Continuing to invest in your expertise, recognising where there are gaps in your knowledge and seeking opportunities to develop expertise in English	By reading this book, you are already engaged in this process! We aim to help you understand more about all aspects of primary English so you can lead with confidence. The 'Questions for reflection' at the end of each chapter are designed to support your personal development.

Adapted from Barker, J., & Rees, T. 'Developing School Leadership', in Lock, S. (ed) *The ResearchEd Guide to Leadership* (C) 2020 John Catt Educational. Reproduced with permission of the Licensor through PLSclear.

Developing your confidence and expertise

This book aims to help you know and understand more about all aspects of primary English so that you can lead with confidence, but we also hope to provide a springboard for you to engage with a wider wealth of guidance and support to enhance your expertise further. In Chapter 2, we offer advice on engaging with research and evidence.

In addition, each chapter features an 'Explore further' section, which signposts further reading or resources to enhance your knowledge in the area of the chapter's focus.

Useful resources

We have set out some additional key documents related to primary English in the table below. You may be familiar with some of these – but, if you are new to leading English, these documents are a great starting point.

USEFUL RESOURCES	LOCATIONS
STATUTORY AND NON-STATUTORY GUIDANCE	
The National Curriculum: Programmes of Study for Key Stages 1 and 2	https://assets.publishing.service.gov.uk/media/5a7de93840f0b62305b7f8ee/PRIMARY_national_curriculum_-_English_220714.pdf
The Early Years Foundation Stage statutory framework: Speech and language guidance	https://assets.publishing.service.gov.uk/media/670fa42a30536cb92748328f/EYFS_statutory_framework_for_group_and_school_-_based_providers.pdf
Development Matters: Information on the links between solid early-years practice and later English learning	https://assets.publishing.service.gov.uk/media/64e6002a20ae890014f26cbc/DfE_Development_Matters_Report_Sep2023.pdf
EVIDENCE SUMMARIES AND REVIEWS	
Guidance from the Education Endowment Foundation (EEF): Evidence-based guidance on the themes of language and literacy bespoke to Key Stages 1 and 2, and resources including a guidance report, summary posters, (which are great for sharing key messages with other staff) and additional tools such as planning templates, case studies and additional evidence	Key Stage 1: https://educationendowmentfoundation.org.uk/education-evidence/guidance-reports/literacy-ks-1 Key Stage 2: https://educationendowmentfoundation.org.uk/education-evidence/guidance-reports/literacy-ks2
Research Review Series: English (Ofsted, 2022): Outline of research relating to the teaching of English National Curriculum aims, considering what progression may enable pupils to meet those aims and exploring linked pedagogy	https://www.gov.uk/government/publications/curriculum-research-review-series-english/curriculum-research-review-series-english
Telling the story: the English education subject report (Ofsted, 2024): Outline of Ofsted's findings on practice in English schools, including recommendations for improvement to the English curriculum	https://www.gov.uk/government/publications/subject-report-series-english/telling-the-story-the-english-education-subject-report

Professional qualifications

You may want to consider undertaking a National Professional Qualification. The NPQ for Leading Teaching is relevant to leaders of all subjects, and the NPQ in Leading Literacy offers a way for you to build some subject-specific expertise. Your school may be eligible for funding if it includes a high proportion of pupils from lower socio-economic backgrounds.

Discussions with colleagues

Exploring and discussing your views with others is a valuable way to develop your knowledge and confidence. Many local authorities, trusts or groups of schools that work informally together organise Teach Meets, study groups and professional development networks for teachers and leaders. Finding out what is available in your local area, or looking to establish a group yourself, could be a helpful way to network with colleagues beyond your school.

> **Case study: developing curricular expertise**
>
> Raheem works in an urban two-form-entry primary school that is part of a small multi-academy trust. He has recently taken on the role of Subject Leader for English. Raheem has a real passion for literature and really wants to offer his pupils the opportunity to develop a love of reading, which is what drove him to take on the role. Raheem realises how complex teaching English is, and decides he wants to develop his thinking about the discipline so he can lead the subject as effectively as possible.
>
> Raheem starts by reading the Ofsted reviews and EEF guides. However, he finds there is a vast amount of information to take in. He realises he would appreciate the opportunity to discuss his response to the reviews with others. He gets in touch with the three other primary school English leads in his trust to ask if they would be interested in setting up a study group. He proposes they read agreed documents in turn, and have conversations focusing on key points and how these might relate to their contexts.

> Over time, the group uses the notes from their discussions to draft and agree a document that outlines their understanding of what makes a good-quality English curriculum. This gives Raheem the confidence to move forwards with shaping a school vision for English teaching that he can articulate to his colleagues.

How this book can support you

Throughout this book, we will explore the varied aspects of the primary English curriculum in more detail, giving you a strong foundation from which to lead the subject. We won't shy away from the complexity of the topics we cover, but we will try to explain things in a clear and easy-to-digest way, and will include plenty of examples drawn from evidence, the views of other experts and our personal experience as teachers and leaders. In this book you will find:

- examples of best practice across key stages
- real and fictional case studies
- suggestions for staff professional development
- reflection questions to help you structure your thoughts and identify next steps
- follow-up reading and resources if you want to explore a particular area further.

In the next chapter, we will draw together insights from cognitive science with evidence related to the practice of English teaching. We will also look at how you can take an evidence-based approach yourself.

We will next move on to look at progression (Chapter 3) and English curriculum design (Chapter 4) before considering how we can best use assessment (Chapter 5).

You will then find detailed chapters on specific areas of the subject: reading (Chapters 6 and 7), writing (Chapter 8), handwriting (Chapter 9), spelling (Chapter 10) and oracy (Chapter 11).

We will finish with some guidance on quality assurance (Chapter 12) and tips on implementing improvement and change (Chapter 13).

Chapter summary

- English is an important subject within the curriculum and our pupils' lives.
- English is a complex subject, but this book intends to help you engage with that complexity to shape a vision for the subject in your school.
- Your role is not only important but also interesting, varied and gratifying. We hope this book can help you enjoy your development in the role.
- This book has been structured to build understanding sequentially, but you can also use the chapter coverage guides at the beginning of chapters, chapter summaries and sub-headings to dip in and out as needed.
- Each chapter of this book has a consistent structure, making it easier for you to navigate.

Questions for reflection

- Do I have a strong sense of what English is as a subject? What makes it different from other areas of the curriculum? Why does it matter?
- Do I think teachers in our school have a shared understanding of the value and purpose of the English curriculum? What could I do to find out? Have I shared my vision for the subject with all colleagues?
- Do our teachers understand the rich interplay between aspects of the English curriculum and the wider curriculum?
- How confident am I in the subject knowledge of the teaching team? Is there any English-specific professional development I would like to source to develop collective expertise?

Explore further

- *Making Meaning in English: Exploring the role of knowledge in the English curriculum* (2021) by David Didau
- *Knowledge in English: Canon, curriculum and cultural literacy* (2020) by Victoria Elliott

- *Primary English Knowledge and Understanding* (2000) by Jane Medwell, George Moore, David Wray and Vivienne Griffiths

Connecting with a wider subject community of English specialists is a great way to grow your expertise. This can be achieved in a number of ways. For example:

- Connecting with colleagues can be a great starting point. Gather teachers together, share and discuss reading related to English teaching and explore how the subject can be contextualised for your setting.
- Start a book group. You could read and discuss class readers, interspersed with papers and books related to the teaching of English.
- Join the thriving English subject community online. English specialists on social media often seek and share advice and resources using #TeamEnglish, and many share blogs and advice.

2 Getting the best from research evidence

As an English subject leader, you could use numerous different types of research to help guide your curriculum design and teaching approaches. However, it can be hard to identify which sources of evidence are likely to be most useful: typing 'literacy research' into an online search engine brings up literally thousands of options. We hope that, by the end of this chapter, you will feel much more confident in navigating the evidence base.

This chapter explores how to use research evidence in two parts:

- First, we look at how to approach research evidence in a productive way.
- We then move on to consider one major field of research: the cognitive science of learning – particularly cognitive load theory and how theory can become applied practice in the classroom, particularly in relation to the English curriculum.

Guiding principles

To implement a new strategy or change effectively as a subject leader, you will need to make evidence-informed decisions. These could draw on both external evidence, such as research, and internal data from your own context about what has and has not worked in the past. The decisions come with an opportunity cost: the more time that is devoted to less effective strategies, the less time there is to spend on more effective ones. Therefore, we need to invest time to select the right solutions. The following approaches can be helpful in guiding decisions.

- **Prioritise large-scale studies**: Focus on research with substantial sample sizes. Leaders are not so interested in how an intervention worked for the pupils within a study; they're interested in whether the same intervention might be beneficial for your own pupils. Bigger samples tend to allow for more generalisable conclusions, leading to interventions appropriate for a wider range of learners.

- **Consider the consistency of the participants**: A large sample size doesn't automatically guarantee high-quality research: you should also examine the participant selection process and drop-out rates. Many reading research studies are conducted on secondary-school pupils and undergraduates so we must be cautious of applying findings about older pupils to those in primary or EYFS. Equally, long-term studies based on primary pupils are prone to changes in participants as pupils and/or teachers move schools.

- **Compare contexts**: If the context of a study is very different from your context, the findings may not be particularly useful. It's worth reading the study parameters carefully to check this. An example of this would be a study that concludes children can learn to read quickly in one year where they begin to learn phonics at age seven. In this study, the children are likely to be learning a language that has a very regular and transparent code that can be learned quickly. To learn English, in comparison, they would need to learn far more code. (In Chapter 6, we explore the reasons behind the complexity of the English language.) Full appreciation of the context would be necessary for the results not to be misleading.

- **Be wary of simplification**: Research that has been distilled into bite-sized chunks can lead us to decisions we believe are perfect fits for our schools. However, we should remember that broadly generalised results, especially those summarised without nuance, can only really give us an 'average effect' impression.

- **Don't trust results implicitly**: We should be mindful that all findings are built on a body of research that can be later refuted as more research studies are published. For example, for many years the EEF (an evidence base discussed below) recommended that, if phonics hadn't worked, a different approach to teaching reading would be necessary. As discussed in Chapter 6, the evidence base strongly indicates that this is not the case and the EEF now does not recommend a different approach.

- **Steer clear of educational fallacies**: The field of education is rife with myths, misconceptions and outdated ideas – for example, that pupils will learn better if they discover things for themselves, or that repetition is the surest way to secure understanding. Many of these persist despite being disproven (de Bruyckere et al., 2015). While you can't be aware of all of the fallacies, familiarising yourself with some common ones can save time, helping you to focus on more-promising approaches. Many are discussed online, in teaching and other literacy forums, and can be sought with a simple search (for example, 'literacy misconceptions'). See the 'Explore further' section for some other suggested reading such as *Urban Myths about Learning and Education* by de Bruyckere, Kirschner & Hulshof (2015) and *The ResearchED Guide to Education Myths: An evidence-informed guide for teachers* (2019), edited by Craig Barton and Tom Bennett.

If you are a subject leader who is new to appraising evidence, you might want to start by looking at the Institute for Effective Education's 'Engaging with evidence guide', which breaks down different types of evidence and their limitations (Haslam & Shaw, 2019). The website 'That's a Claim!' (www.thatsaclaim.org/educational) is also helpful for bitesize explainers on different aspects of educational research.

Primary education sources and guidance

There are several notable challenges that make accessing, analysing and interpreting evidence difficult for those of us who work in schools. Lack of time to read and digest research, and difficulty interpreting the scientific jargon in research papers, are challenges familiar to many of us.

A good starting point is to look at what organisations who commission and conduct research have found to be effective. These organisations often digest research for educators into more-accessible formats and collate research into summaries.

While keeping the guiding principles in mind, you may find the following evidence bases useful.

The Education Endowment Foundation (EEF)

The EEF is an independent charity that was set up to improve educational attainment levels of pupils from lower socio-economic backgrounds in

England. The Foundation helps schools, colleges and Early Years settings improve outcomes through the better use of evidence. This may be through their guidance reports, which review the evidence base for a range of strategies developed to support specific areas. Alternatively, it may be through research into the efficacy of specific strategies.

- Their guidance reports *Improving Literacy in Key Stage 1* (Higgins et al., 2020), *Improving Literacy in Key Stage 2* (2021) and *Preparing for Literacy* (2021) are productive starting points for English leads.
- The *Teaching and Learning Toolkit* (2021) is also helpful when thinking about curriculum and lesson design, as well as how to support teachers to become more effective in their practice.
- *A School's Guide to Implementation* (2024) provides clear structures and systems that can help us when implementing new strategies in our schools.

The Chartered College of Teaching

The Chartered College of Teaching is a professional body for teachers. Membership gives access to research, resources and the journal *Impact*. The College produces evidence summaries that review and collate research into short digests, and the journal has regular contributions from practitioners as well as researchers.

English-specific resources

Subject associations and local networks are useful gateways for staying up to date with emerging research and discourse within the subject. They also offer training and guidance on the teaching of English at primary school level.

ASSOCIATIONS	LOCATIONS
The English Association offers support, teaching resources and networking opportunities for colleagues in primary and Early Years education.	https://englishassociation.ac.uk/
The National Association of Teachers of English offers publications and training for English teachers at all key stages.	https://www.nate.org.uk/
The National Literacy Trust is a charity focused on supporting children, young people and adults with the literacy skills they need to succeed.	https://literacytrust.org.uk/
The UK Literacy Association provides PD guidance, and research focused on language, literacy and communication.	https://ukla.org/
English Hubs promote a love of reading and support schools in providing excellent phonics and early language teaching, through tailored support.	https://www.gov.uk/government/publications/english-hubs-list-of-primary-schools
ResearchED is a grassroots organisation that aims to bridge the gap between research and practice in education. It brings together researchers, teachers and policy makers at conferences, which often feature subject focused sessions. The organisation also publishes short books with chapters from many of the speakers. The ResearchED guides to Literacy, Primary English, Leadership and Direct and Explicit Instruction, for example, are very useful for us as English leads.	https://researched.org.uk/

Social media, blogs and podcasts

Social media platforms offer helpful starting points for engaging with researchers and school-based practitioners. Podcasts can help you absorb information while 'on the go', and blogs can provide useful sources of practical advice and research papers.

USEFUL RESOURCES	LOCATIONS
SOCIAL MEDIA PLATFORMS	
BlueSky	#EduSky #PrimaryEduSky #Team English
X (formerly Twitter)	#edutwitter #Team English
PODCASTS	
Thinking Deeply About Primary Education: Researchers and teachers discuss teaching, learning, pedagogy, knowledge, curriculum and all things education.	https://www.youtube.com/@TDaPE and available on most streaming platforms
Science of Reading: the Podcast: Each episode takes a conversational approach and explores a timely topic related to reading.	https://amplify.com/science-of-reading-the-podcast/
The Evidence Based Education Podcast: Hosts discuss key issues in the field of evidence-based education, particularly focusing on how gaps between policy, research and practice can be bridged.	https://evidencebased.education/podcast-archive/ and available on most streaming platforms
Mind the Gap: The hosts interview experts from the UK, US and beyond to share timely insights on trends for Early Years to Year 13, research-based approaches in need of greater reach and strategies to close global gaps.	https://www.youtube.com/c/mindthegapwithtomemma (Also available on most streaming platforms.)

USEFUL RESOURCES	LOCATIONS
BLOGS	
The Reading Ape: A series of blogs explore the teaching of reading.	https://www.thereadingape.com/
Shanahan on Literacy: The site features blogs and resources related to the teaching of reading.	https://www.shanahanonliteracy.com/
The 3Rs: The site provides resources and access to a fortnightly newsletter discussing writing, reading and research from the world of education.	https://alexquigley.co.uk/

What does the research say about cognitive science?

It's crucial for all subject leads and teachers to have a solid grasp of cognitive science and to stay current with its research findings on learning processes. These insights should be the foundation for all our teaching and learning strategies. In this next section, we outline key points all teachers need to understand and then provide worked examples linked to teaching the English curriculum. In particular we hope the worked examples will demonstrate how knowledge of cognitive load theory helps us ensure children remember their learning over time.

In his book *Why Don't Students Like School?* (2021), D. T. Willingham draws on the simple model of memory propounded by A. D. Baddeley and G. Hitch (1974). He explains the theoretical model and its impact for teaching in the classroom.

Here's a concise overview:

- **Working memory** acts as our brain's processing centre, briefly holding small amounts of new information. On average, an adult can hold and actively process about four chunks of new information in their working memory at a time. For children, it's likely to be fewer.
- **Learning** occurs when we successfully move new information from working memory into long-term memory.
- **Cognitive overload** can hinder or halt learning if working memory becomes overwhelmed. This happens when we're faced with too much new information to process simultaneously.
- **Optimising load** means reducing cognitive load that's unrelated to new key learning (such as new rules for a game) in order to increase capacity for essential cognitive load. This could be assisted by linking new content with information already stored in long-term memory, as this doesn't take up lots of space in working memory.
- **Long-term memory** organises and stores information in structures called 'schemas'. These schemas can range from simple, containing just a few pieces of information, to highly complex, encompassing a vast quantity of data. The capacity of long-term memory may be finite.

Once information is stored in the long-term memory, it is accessed by the process of retrieval. All teachers should also be familiar with research on retrieval practice, as explained, for example, by Pashler et al. (2007):

- **Frequent recall** of learned material can enhance pupils' retention. The act of retrieving information reinforces the information in memory and reduces the likelihood of forgetting.
- **Spaced retrieval** is the most effective form of retrieval. Retrieval is most effective when pupils have started to forget the material: this requires more mental effort during recall, thereby strengthening memory connections. For optimal results, retrieval practice should be spread out over time rather than concentrated in a single session.

This research helps us to understand how learning occurs and has several implications for the classroom:

- **Implementing targeted planning**: Pupils need to concentrate on essential knowledge, skills and concepts. Teachers should be directed and assisted to design activities that direct pupils' focus to these core elements.
- **Building on existing knowledge**: Pupils understand new ideas by relating them to what they already know. Planning should be shaped by assessing and building upon pupils' prior knowledge.
- **Managing cognitive demands**: Pupils' working memory can easily become overwhelmed with new information. Teachers should be guided in how to be mindful of the cognitive load they impose, and plans should introduce new material in manageable segments.
- **Fostering fluency**: To develop deep understanding and fluency, pupils need to revisit and apply important content regularly. Plans should include spaced practice: frequent reviews, retrieval tasks and ample opportunities for pupils to apply what they've learned.
- **Adjusting support levels**: As pupils develop a more-sophisticated understanding in a subject area, they require less guidance. Teachers should be encouraged to assess pupil understanding continuously and be allowed the flexibility to adjust their levels of support accordingly, matching it to pupils' growing expertise.

Building background knowledge

Building vocabulary knowledge is probably the most impactful thing we can do to build pupils' background knowledge. The more vocabulary they have, the easier it is for them to join in conversations, understand what they are reading and express themselves in their writing.

In the 1990s, B. Hart and T. R. Risley published a study identifying that children in the households of professionals heard on average 11 million words a year, in comparison to approximately three million words for children in families claiming welfare support (1995). This study was the first of its kind to link vocabulary size to socio-economic status explicitly. Its methodology has been widely critiqued (see Shanahan, 2018 for a helpful summary), and subsequent studies have not identified as large a gap, but they have all reported noticeable vocabulary gaps in their overall findings (Fernald, Marchman, & Weisleder, 2013). However, as Alex Quigley argues, further research prompted from Hart and Risley's original work has taught us that early language exposure matters (Quigley, 2022).

Children who have not had plentiful exposure to rich language may find it difficult to engage with the more-academic language used in schools, whereas children who have heard a lot of rich, discursive language are more likely to experience this academic language at home. J. Law et al. identified in their research that pupils with language difficulties upon entry to Year 1 are four times more likely to have reading difficulties in adulthood than those who don't (Law, et al., 2017).

In Chapters 6 and 7, on reading, we explore the important role of vocabulary instruction for reading. In Chapter 11, on oracy, we reflect on the importance of discrete vocabulary teaching to develop oracy from Early Years Foundation Stages (EYFS) to the end of Key Stage 2.

Vocabulary development in your context

We suggest reflecting on and discussing these findings with the EYFS lead in your school. Are you seeing pupils joining you in Early Years with less well-developed vocabulary than in previous years? Is it all pupils or groups? What impact is this having on their ability to access your curriculum?

Implications for the classroom

The research evidence for how learning happens demonstrates that we need to always think about how we can reduce the load on working memory when introducing new learning. Very often, gaps in children's learning happen because teachers have moved through the curriculum too quickly. They may not give enough examples of a new concept to help children build their schema around it or they may not revisit learning over time through spaced retrieval. Using worked examples is a very useful way to build children's schema by linking new learning to their existing background knowledge. In our writing chapter, we outline why writing is such a cognitively challenging process. The case studies below are linked to writing to show how two teachers address common errors by planning learning sequences that take account of cognitive load theory. These case studies show how two teachers use worked examples to build background knowledge and allow for spaced practice in their writing lessons.

Case study: worked examples to build knowledge of sentences

Freya teaches a Year 2 English class in Peterborough. Many of the pupils speak in incomplete sentences (fragments) and, for many of them, English is not a first language. At the beginning of the year, Freya notices that many of her pupils do not know the difference between full sentences and fragments. She works with the school's English lead to build a teaching sequence to address this.

- Freya focuses on statements as the most basic variety of sentences. She explains that they consist of two parts: a subject (who or what the sentence is about) and a predicate (the words that contain the verb and tell us what the subject is doing, feeling or being).
- She shows examples of statements using content from the curriculum and annotates the two parts under a visualiser. She repeats this for several lessons to build pupils' mental models of simple statements from across the curriculum. Using her knowledge of cognitive load theory, Freya knows that repeating this learning over time will help all children to internalise that a sentence contains two parts.
- Once children have built their schema around simple sentences in a range of contexts, Freya provides a selection of statements and fragments and asks the pupils to identify the fragments. She models 'fixing' the fragments by adding the subject/predicate. She keeps the structure the same as the complete sentences she used earlier in the sequence. This means they have enough free space in their working memory to 'fix' the fragments. She does this repeatedly over a series of lessons using the principles of spaced practice to help transfer this knowledge into long-term memory.
- When the pupils are confident identifying the fragments, Freya gives them examples to identify and fix orally. As children become competent at this, Freya is able to lengthen the spaced practice.

Case study: worked examples to build cohesion across sentences

Juan teaches a combined class of pupils in Years 3 and 4 in a school in Wisbech. His Year 4 pupils are not linking paragraphs using fronted adverbials as cohesive devices (such as 'Firstly', 'Consequently' or 'The following day'). Juan knows from cognitive load theory that it is important to reduce the load on working memory by introducing new learning in small steps and linking it to existing knowledge. He therefore addresses the problem as follows.

- After modelling the use of the fronted adverbials 'Firstly' and 'Next' for the Year 3 pupils, and asking them to write pairs of sentences beginning with them, Juan works with the Year 4 pupils.
- He has pre-prepared two linking sentences to model writing. Both sentences begin with adverbials – 'Suddenly' and 'In response' – which have been encountered by the pupils previously, so they are only focusing on how to use them as cohesive devices.
- As he writes the first sentence, he discusses his thinking and decision-making.
- He repeats this with the second sentence.
- He draws pupils' attention to the impact of the devices, and how they changed the meaning of the sentences. He then asks the Year 4 pupils to say a sentence that uses one of the adverbials to a partner.
- After taking feedback to check for misconceptions, he repeats the process with the second adverbial.
- He provides the pupils with a series of statements closely linked to his worked examples, and asks them to select the most appropriate fronted adverbial for each statement.
- Knowing learning happens over time, Juan plans to give the Year 4 pupils a range of adverbials to link a range of sentences over the rest of the week, to continue to build their mental models. By doing this, he is building their background knowledge so they can link this new learning to existing knowledge.

Chapter summary

- There is a range of evidence bases we can use to navigate our way through the debates surrounding English and to inform our planning and teaching.
- When evaluating research, we should focus on large-scale studies with consistency of participants, be sure to consider studies' contexts, be wary of simplification and the fallibility of researchers, and be aware of common educational myths and misconceptions.
- Learning is a cognitive process. Key insights from cognitive science help us understand the process of learning and, importantly, how these can be applied to teaching English.
- Perhaps the most-important factor of applying cognitive-science principles in the classroom is the augmentation of prior knowledge.

Questions for reflection

- How do I use research evidence to help inform curriculum choices?
- In what ways am I currently considering my school context and the research evidence when implementing new teaching strategies?
- How confidently could I explain cognitive load theory? What do I want to explore further?
- How well does our English curriculum support learning and progression, based on what we know about cognitive load theory?
- How well do staff understand the limits of working memory?
- Do all staff understand the evidence base for and importance of teaching vocabulary?

Example PD session: building background knowledge

You could conduct a PD session on building background knowledge as follows:

TIMING SUGGESTION	SESSION GUIDANCE
10 mins	Use the section on cognitive science research to explain to colleagues the importance of building background knowledge in English lessons.
15 mins	<ul><li>Ask a colleague to describe a scenario in which a pupil (or group of pupils) either did not achieve a learning goal or said the learning was boring.</li><li>Elicit the learning points covered in the lesson, and discuss whether all pupils are likely to have had sufficient background knowledge before starting the learning.</li><li>Discuss which components may have been missing, and what could have been included in the teaching sequence.</li><li>Repeat with other scenarios as necessary.</li></ul>
10 mins	Prompt colleagues to consider their learning sequence for next week:<ul><li>Are there any background component steps on which they need to spend more time?</li><li>Do they need to build knowledge in advance for particular pupils?</li></ul>

Explore further

- *The ResearchED Guide to Explicit and Direct Instruction* (2019) edited by Adam Boxer
- *How Learning Happens: Seminal works in educational psychology and what they mean* (2020) by Paul Kirschner and Carl Hendrick
- The Learning Scientists' podcast: https://www.learningscientists.org/podcast-episodes

- *Understanding How We Learn* (2019) by Yana Weinstein and Megan Sumeracki, with Oliver Caviglioli
- *Why Don't Students Like School?* (2021) by Daniel Willingham
- *Urban Myths about Learning and Education* by de Bruyckere, Kirschner & Hulshof (2015) and *The ResearchED Guide to Education Myths: An evidence-informed guide for teachers* (2019), edited by Craig Barton and Tom Bennett.

3 Progression in English

> Pupils will benefit from a curriculum that has considered how pupils learn (see Chapter 2) alongside content that is essential for gaining proficiency in English (see Chapter 4). Therefore, this chapter asks: how we can conceptualise the idea of progress in English? We will cover:
>
> - the 'components before composites' approach to English planning and teaching
> - the meaning of 'understanding' and how it relates to the organisation and transfer of knowledge
> - how we can build pupil expertise over time
> - the importance of texts chosen for study.

Common problems with a focus on outcomes

It is not unusual to see progression maps for primary-level English that focus most explicitly on outcomes: the performance of skills that pupils are expected to master. For example, within a typical reading curriculum, we may see a progression map that features the following.

YEAR 3	YEAR 4	YEAR 5	YEAR 6
Demonstrate enjoyment of reading	Demonstrate enjoyment of reading	Demonstrate enjoyment of reading	Demonstrate enjoyment of reading
Compare a range of texts	Participate in discussions and compare a wide range of texts	Continue to demonstrate understanding by discussing an increasingly wide range of texts	Explain understanding of a text through discussion

YEAR 3	YEAR 4	YEAR 5	YEAR 6
Retrieve information from a text	Identify the main ideas from a text	Retrieve, record and present information	Use retrieval skills, e.g. skimming

Whilst these outcomes are desirable, the map doesn't tell us what we need to teach. What are the building blocks that will improve pupil performance? How might we *teach* a pupil to enjoy reading? How would this look different in Year 6 or Year 5? What's the difference between retrieving information in Year 3 and using retrieval skills in Year 6?

This type of overview can lead to a curriculum in which pupils each year are repeating the same or similar activities, led by a teacher who hopes they will produce an improved, more-sophisticated or more-complex outcome. It is not uncommon to visit a range of year groups across primary classrooms and see pupils being asked to do essentially the same things: 'Today, we are answering inference questions'; 'I'd like you to write a story opening that focuses on describing settings'; 'Let's look at retrieving information from a text'. In such a model, it is hard to see how pupils are being equipped with the specific tools they need to make progress.

Practice plays an important role in learning, but we need to be clear about exactly *what* pupils need to practise if they are to improve their performance. Too often, we focus on producing outcomes that demonstrate the use of skills; this means we miss the opportunity to teach and let pupils practise the individual building blocks that make up those skills.

Components of English

These building blocks can be considered as components that can be put together in different ways. The products of combined and structured components are composites. If we take a 'components before composites' rather than composite-driven approach, we focus on teaching, giving pupils time to practise, and then assessing, the specific components that pupils need in order to perform well in English.

This approach is supported by current understanding of what happens when we learn: our working memory must hold information before it transfers to long-term memory, and can process only a certain amount at a time. Because our pupils are novice learners, we must remember that their working memory capacity will be less developed than our own and can therefore be easily overwhelmed. This is especially true in relation to reading and writing, which demand that we engage with many different areas of knowledge at once.

We therefore need to support our pupils in building those rich webs of knowledge. To do so, we need to break composites down into their component parts and provide pupils with plenty of opportunities to practise. Over time, we will enable them to combine and recombine their component knowledge into varied composites, demonstrating their growing proficiency in English.

One perspective we can take when considering progress in English is to ask whether our pupils are mastering a growing body of component knowledge. As they acquire components necessary for reading, writing and talking, they should be able to read increasingly complex texts, write with increasing sophistication and talk with increasing confidence.

Example - components of oracy

Identifying component knowledge can difficult. As an example of how this can be done, let's think for a moment about the components we might need in order to support pupils in becoming effective users of spoken language. They could be broken down as:

- voice control (volume, pace tone)
- body language
- eye contact
- vocabulary
- grammatical constructions
- use of rhetorical devices
- organisation of ideas
- content knowledge (what we will talk about)
- tailoring talk to purpose and audience
- noticing and attending to listeners' non-verbal feedback
- turn taking
- framing disagreement
- referring to and building on the ideas of others
- signifying agreement

All these elements could be broken down into yet smaller building blocks, which are discussed in Chapter 11. Chapters 6–8 will help you consider and map components that form the composites of reading and writing.

Building understanding in English

Another approach to considering pupil progress is to consider the extent to which they *understand* something. Often, teachers talk about pupils' 'understanding' as distinct from 'knowing': understanding is associated with being able to put knowledge to use, and it is not uncommon to see differentiated lesson outcomes. For example:

- All pupils will know what a simile is.
- Most pupils understand how a writer uses similes in a text.
- Some pupils will be able to write their own simile.

It is likely that, once taught a simple definition, many pupils will be able to repeat back to a teacher that a simile is a comparison using 'like' or 'as'. It is likely that they will be able to identify similes that follow familiar structures (such as 'x is like y' or 'x is as y as z'). They may also be able to produce their own lists of similes, particularly if given a sentence-starter prompt like 'It was as white as …'.

At this point, we may feel confident that we have taught a necessary component related to developing pupils' skills as readers and evaluators of literature. Using the terms of the outcomes above, we may believe that pupils' ability to identify and write similes proves they have understood the concept. In the future, however, we may find that pupils fail to notice and comment on the effects of similes, and that their own uses of similes are formulaic, clunky and ineffective.

This is because, although we have taken the time to identify and teach a piece of component knowledge, one lesson is not enough to move pupils beyond shallow knowledge.

To grasp this, rather than seeing 'knowing' and 'understanding' as distinct, we can recognise them as the same thing, and view learning as a process that deepens knowledge by making connections between new learning and what is already known (Willingham, 2009). It is not that some things involve knowing and others involve understanding, but that everything must be known and then understood.

This idea should feed into teaching plans. When pupils are first introduced to similes, they may be given a simple definition. This could then be the focus of retrieval quizzes and regular checks that pupils are able to recite the definition. However, unless pupils are able to connect this definition to an example, we would consider this rote learning. They have just memorised a definition.

Following this, pupils can be provided with some examples, perhaps from a particular book already enjoyed by the class. This will enable pupils to connect their understanding of similes to familiar examples: this would be an example of shallow or inflexible knowledge. The knowledge is so closely attached to the old ideas that pupils are unable to recognise the concept in a new context – they may point out all the similes in the familiar book, but fail to recognise similes in a new text or in a non-fiction text.

If pupils are ever to reach a point at which they independently analyse and use similes to good effect, they will need to see multiple concrete examples, beginning with familiar ones so you can build on their prior learning. They must also, then, be involved in rich discussions of their effect. This would forge deep or flexible knowledge, characterised by interconnected knowledge that enables pupils to make true sense of what they have been taught.

Shallow, inflexible knowledge is the norm when we are first learning (Willingham, 2002), so this process takes time. Rather than rushing through curriculum content, we should recognise that inflexible knowledge is a necessary part of the learning process and needs to be developed. Pupils will need to encounter and discuss the effect of similes in a wide range of texts, including their own writing, if they are to develop the deep knowledge we want them to attain.

In practice: building deep knowledge of similes

Over the course of a curriculum, the process of developing deep knowledge of similes may look like the example below.

- The first time pupils encounter this concept within the curriculum, the teacher introduces a simple definition and asks pupils to repeat it back. They then draw pupils' attention to the use of similes in a familiar text, for example a book shared in class. In this way, pupils are invited to notice and name a particular feature with which they are familiar but perhaps hadn't considered before. Pupils talk about the similes and their effects.
- As pupils progress, teachers regularly check that the definition of 'simile' is secure. This may be done through retrieval quizzes planned throughout the

English curriculum, but should also be done whenever a reading or writing lesson involves similes.

- Teachers draw pupils' attention to the use of similes in a wide range of fiction and non-fiction texts read throughout primary school. They take the time to talk with pupils about the effects of the similes. In this way, the teacher is drawing on information from pupils' long-term memory and also building on these ideas through multiple examples.
- In writing lessons, pupils are given plenty of opportunities to use and consider the effectiveness of similes in their own writing. For example:
  - The teacher shares an example simile and the class discusses why the author may have made particular choices.
  - The teacher introduces a focus noun for a simile. The class suggests and discusses different adjectives that could be associated with this focus, considering both positive and negative associations. This could be supported through the use of images carefully selected by the teacher.
  - The class is challenged to think of other nouns that share some properties with the original focus.
  - The teacher models using these comparisons to write similes on the board. Pupils are asked to describe the impact of each choice.
  - Pupils write their own similes and discuss them with partners, exploring their impact and what works best in the context of their writing.

The importance of text choice

A further way to interpret progress is to consider whether pupils are reading and writing increasingly sophisticated texts. Reading literature is fundamental to the English curriculum: nothing provides a better induction to the subject (Didau et al., 2024). Particularly for those pupils without exposure to fiction and poetry outside of school, the English subject lead has the incredibly important job of curating pupils' early experience of literature.

Reading texts takes time, so you need to ensure your timetable and curriculum map give plenty of time for reading and responding to texts in full.

What are we inadvertently teaching pupils about the value of literature if we repeatedly run out of time to finish a book?

This is even more likely to be an issue if teachers feel under pressure to have written work completed in each lesson. In such a situation, the time to read and talk can be rushed through, in order to get something down on paper. The desire to provide evidence of progress can actually get in the way of genuine learning. At times, of course, written outcomes are desirable and can be useful for the assessment of pupils' understanding. However, plenty of reading and discussion are the elements of the lesson that are most supportive of pupils' progress (Such, 2021, p. 131). We will offer more guidance on the balance between monitoring and promoting learning in Chapter 12.

You will want to consider how the texts pupils read in lessons deal with increasingly complex ideas and prepare them for more challenging reading later on. You will also want to offer texts that expand pupils' horizons, offering them worlds and views that are distant from their own, whilst encountering protagonists and heroes that are similar to themselves. If a purpose of literature is to explore the human condition by connecting the individual to wider humanity, reading a range of texts that express diverse truths *is* making progress.

Throughout, your overarching goal should be ensuring understanding and promoting enjoyment. Remember, pupils are going to enjoy reading only if they are able to participate with fluency and expression. Mastery of the components of reading are key to this. Chapters 6 and 7 will support you in balancing the mechanics of reading with considerations of progression in text choice and complexity.

Chapter summary

- Progress in English can be considered as:
  - mastering a growing body of component knowledge.
  - moving from shallow knowledge to deep understanding, which enables pupils to transfer their learning to new and different contexts.
  - reading and understanding a range of texts that increase in complexity and express diverse truths.

- Pupils need to be exposed to multiple examples of concepts and have plentiful opportunity to practise using them.
- Subject leaders can aim to specify, in precise detail, the component knowledge that they want pupils to learn.
- Careful consideration of what texts to specify in a reading scheme can aid pupils' progress towards both comprehending and enjoying increasingly complex writing.

Questions for reflection

- How specific and focused on components is the teaching of reading, writing and oracy at our school? Am I confident that all teachers understand the components to be taught, and how these fit into the whole school curriculum for English?
- Is reading time protected in our school? How do I ensure pupils are exposed to a wide range of diverse and quality texts?
- How well understood are the learning goals of our English curriculum? What distractions may prevent teachers from focusing on this goal?

Explore further

Deep learning, or the movement from inflexible to flexible knowledge, is explained clearly in Daniel T. Willingham's 'Inflexible Knowledge: The First Step to Expertise' in the *American Educator* section 'Ask the Cognitive Scientist': https://www.aft.org/ae/winter2002/willingham.

4 Curriculum design

> Having considered what progress means in English, in this chapter we turn our attention to curriculum design: a key element of your role as subject leader. In this chapter, we will:
>
> - explore what a curriculum is and the types of knowledge that make up how we see and think in English
> - build understanding of the importance of sequencing curriculum content, incorporating different approaches to aspects of knowledge in English
> - consider how we may need to adapt our planning if we have mixed-age classes
> - further explore the importance of text choice, now considering the breadth of texts chosen
> - consider the importance of ensuring all teachers are familiar with long-term goals, past learning and how their teaching fits into the whole school curriculum.

What is a curriculum?

A curriculum sets out what we want pupils to learn. You are likely to be familiar with the terms 'intent', 'implementation' and 'impact' with regards to curriculum planning, and unpicking these terms can provide a useful frame for articulating the curriculum.

- **Intent** is what you intend to teach. What are the topics, ideas and concepts that you want pupils to learn? To determine this, you will draw on your knowledge of the subject alongside your knowledge of your pupils and school context. This should be mapped out and sequenced into a top-level overview.
- **Implementation** is *how* teachers will teach the curriculum. It includes both subject-specific pedagogy and resources such as the schemes, lesson plans, worksheets, slideshows, planned explanations, expositions

and questions. Implementation is how the curriculum comes to life. It is how plans translate into classroom practice, and relates directly to the pupils' actual experience of the curriculum. This will be discussed further in Chapters 6–11.

- **Impact** is the learning that results from the curriculum. This will be covered in more detail in Chapter 5.

Planning the curriculum begins with intent. This chapter explores your role in overseeing what will be taught, and sequencing knowledge to build pupil learning.

Ways of knowing in English

In her book *Curriculum: Theory, culture and the subject specialisms* (2021), school leader Ruth Ashbee encourages us to acknowledge that knowledge exists in various forms, each with unique characteristics. She suggests that understanding the nature of knowledge within different subjects enhances our comprehension of those subjects (Ashbee, 2021, p. 39). How, then, might we categorise the nature of knowledge relevant to the English curriculum? The table below suggests ways we might summarise these categories, provides some examples from English and explains their relevance to the English curriculum.

TYPE OF KNOWLEDGE	DEFINITION	EXAMPLES IN ENGLISH	CONSIDERATIONS
Declarative knowledge Knowing *that*…	Knowledge that can be articulated, such as facts, ideas or opinions	• The alphabetic code • Subject terms such as 'alliteration' • Text structures and conventions	This knowledge can be captured in a knowledge organiser, and is commonly tested through retrieval quizzes.

TYPE OF KNOWLEDGE	DEFINITION	EXAMPLES IN ENGLISH	CONSIDERATIONS
Procedural or non-declarative knowledge Knowing *how*…	The knowledge necessary to carry out and complete processes	• Segmentation and blending of sounds in phonics • Construction of a range of sentence types • Use of tentative language for exploring meaning within analytical paragraphs	This essentially equates to skills. If practised enough, procedural knowledge can become tacit; this means we can perform a procedure without conscious thought. It's worth knowing that our own tacit knowledge can lead to the 'curse of the expert': the more unconscious a process has become, the harder it is to identify and teach the component parts. An example of this is decoding within reading: when we see text, we decode it automatically. Most of us, therefore, need a phonics scheme to guide us in breaking down how to teach it. Procedural knowledge often depends on declarative knowledge. For example, to segment and blend sounds (to separate sounds in a word and to run them together), you need to know the sound–spelling correspondences.

TYPE OF KNOWLEDGE	DEFINITION	EXAMPLES IN ENGLISH	CONSIDERATIONS
Disciplinary knowledge Knowing how to work within a subject	Knowledge of how to work within the conventions or rules of a subject to establish and contest ideas, involving ways of working in a specific discipline	• Attentiveness to textual detail • Analysis and interpretation of texts • Establishment of meaning through discourse • Composition of well-crafted texts	In responding to texts, knowledge in English is constructed through a process of claims and counter-claims. Knowing how to participate in this process is disciplinary knowledge for English. This contrasts with the disciplinary knowledge involved in a subject like science, which is constructed through empirical research.
Substantive knowledge Knowing how a subject relates to the world	Knowledge about the wider claims or truths established within a subject, which are refined and critiqued over time and lead to varied perspectives	• Exploration of how Shakespeare's *Macbeth* is concerned with the damaging impact of personal ambition • Identification that Gothic literature reflects and explores the repressed fears of society	In certain subjects, for example science, substantive knowledge is taught to pupils as established. English is different. From an early age, pupils are invited to consider, contest and contribute to substantive knowledge by sharing their own views and ideas. This is because the goal of English is not consensus, but interpretation. This does not, however, mean English is a free-for-all with no wrong answers. It is important we guide pupils to reach views by working in a disciplinary way: referring to textual detail, for example, rather than making wild claims.

NB: Developed skills are cumulative. For example, in order to develop the disciplinary knowledge needed for evaluation of substantive-knowledge claims, pupils will draw on both declarative knowledge (knowledge of text, structure, context, grammar and linguistic devices) and procedural or non-declarative knowledge (analysis of said features and their use in the text to make meaning).

These concepts offer a framework for considering more deeply the ways we see and think in English. They could better equip you to consider curricular questions in a way that both respects the subject and bears pupil's accumulation of knowledge in mind. By appreciating how they relate uniquely to English, you could also draw on them to deepen your knowledge of the discipline, helping you to grow as a subject leader.

Sequencing knowledge

When sequencing a curriculum, an important question to ask is this: 'What do pupils need to learn if they are to access future learning?'

Within a more hierarchical subject, the logical progression of knowledge is more obvious. Maths is often given as an example of a hierarchical subject. Consider, for example, how a pupil would benefit from a secure sense of number before being introduced to fractions. In a hierarchical subject, close attention to sequencing is very important as gaps can leave a long-lasting impact if not dealt with (see Figure 4.1).

A cumulative subject, on the other hand, does not have such an obvious pathway. History is often given as an example of a cumulative subject, because there is less consensus over which topics must be studied and in which order.

The reality is that most subjects fall somewhere on a spectrum. Even within a subject, some aspects may have a more obvious hierarchical or cumulative nature than others. In English, we may consider the teaching of the alphabetic code and grammar to be more hierarchical in nature, whilst the study of literature can develop in a more-cumulative fashion.

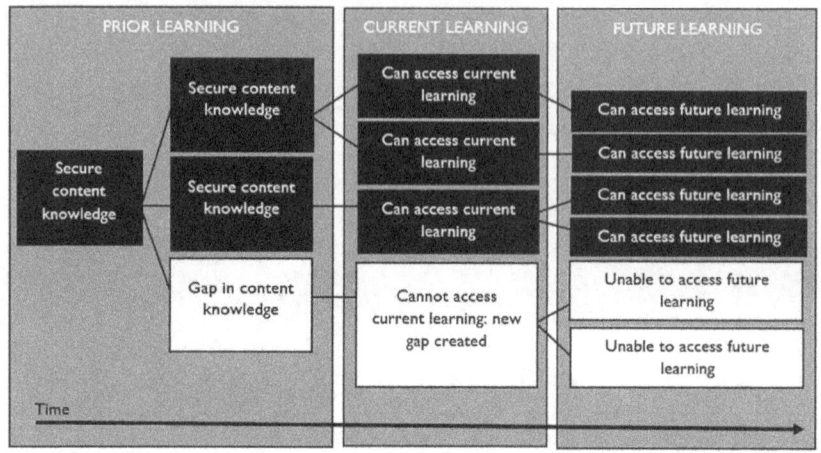

Figure 4.1: A hierarchical curriculum and the relationship to learning over time

Ashbee suggests that, when sequencing our curriculums, we ask ourselves which strands of knowledge are impacted by order *most crucially*. We can then sequence appropriately. When considering what knowledge can build more cumulatively, we can sequence more flexibly (Ashbee, 2021, p. 56).

To make the process of sequencing your English curriculum more manageable, you may find it useful to group aspects of the subject into broad areas. You can then sequence within these areas rather than attempting to manage all strands at once.

First things first: phonics as curriculum content

Knowledge of the alphabetic code is essential in learning to read and, consquently, selecting a phonics scheme for your school should be a priority. Some primary teachers talk of phonics as a 'method' for teaching reading, and may contest that there are alternative methods that can be as effective – or more so. This is a fundamental misconception: phonics is not a method, but a combination of foundational declarative and procedural knowledge that needs to be taught. An example of the foundations it provides for reading is shown in the table below.

TYPE OF KNOWLEDGE	EXAMPLE
Declarative	In the word 'play', the spelling 'ay' represents the /eɪ/ sound.
Procedural	• Pupils segment the word 'play' into individual sounds: /p/ /l/ /eɪ/. • Pupils blend the sounds to say the word.

You can see why we need to teach this content knowledge early: this is essential curriculum content that enables pupils to learn to read any text. You will find more consideration of this in Chapter 6, on early reading, including guidance as to what to look for when selecting a phonics scheme.

Organising knowledge in English: an example

In the primary schools we lead, we have chosen to organise the different areas of the curriculum as follows.

- reading progression
- word structure and spelling
- transcription
- sentence structure, incorporating:
  - grammar
  - types of sentences
  - punctuation
- oracy
- text structure, incorporating:
  - fiction
  - non-fiction

- composition, incorporating:
  - analysis
  - language devices
  - vocabulary

Each year group has specified component knowledge and accompanying key terminology under each of these headings. We have then thought carefully about sequencing within each area: for example, pupils must be secure with phrases and clauses before we begin work on complex sentences or tenses. Our progression documents clarify what the expected outcomes or learning indicators are for each year group, and these are firmly connected to the content we have explicitly taught.

You will probably find that, rather than a step-by-step process, mapping out your curriculum feels like you are constantly zooming in and out of the detail. You will likely move between thinking about very specific things you'd like pupils to learn, stepping back to identify broad areas to organise that knowledge, zooming in again to identify and sequence components within that area, and stepping back again to check how it fits together.

This can feel a bit messy, but don't worry: gradually, you will start to see structure emerging in your plans. We offer much more specific detail to support you with this process in each of the relevant chapters on reading, writing and oracy.

Organising texts

Alongside the organisation of ideas discussed above, a further consideration for you as an English subject leader is text selection. Once you have identified the core concepts you wish to cover in the curriculum, you can consider which texts will enable pupils to encounter and re-encounter these concepts and ideas progressively, in increasingly complex and sophisticated ways. You will recognise how helpful it is to specify which books your pupils will read. Without this, collective understanding of how the components of English can be taught in relation to texts becomes difficult to manage.

When identifying suitable texts, you will also want to think about the increasing level of challenge presented by the stories, novels, poetry and non-fiction teachers read with pupils. One of the purposes of education is to enable pupils to do things they could not manage without our teaching. Related to this is the idea that pupils should be supported to read texts that are more ambitious and challenging than those they could reasonably be expected to read independently. When it comes to novels, it is also important that pupils are supported to experience whole books rather than only extracts.

Over time, a good English curriculum will ensure pupils are exposed to a range of texts that:

- are interesting, entertaining and enjoyable stories
- are worthy of study within the planned curriculum
- support the concepts you have elected to teach within your curriculum
- build cultural literacy (for example, contrasting classic children's literature with high-quality contemporary fiction)
- expose pupils to a diverse range of authentic voices, building on their capacity to see their place in the world and to connect with the experiences of others from a range of backgrounds, time periods and cultures.

Selecting the texts with which your pupils engage may be one of the most important contributions you make in preparing them for success in secondary English.

At the time of writing, the National Curriculum for GCSE English Literature demands that pupils must study, in full, a Shakespeare text, a nineteenth-century novel, post-1914 prose fiction or drama and a collection of poetry written between the eighteenth century and today. Lemov, Driggs and Woolway (2016) identify five difficulties that these kinds of complex text present:

- archaic language
- non-linear time sequences
- complexity of narrator/narration
- complex storytelling (plot and symbolism)
- resistant text: text that is playful or experimental in its use of conventional storytelling, often because it is communicating ideas that are, in themselves, challenging to convey.

To prepare pupils well for such challenging reads, Lemov et al. suggest the introduction of what they term 'pre-complex' texts. This does not mean the primary curriculum should be stuffed full of the kinds of texts pupils will read at secondary school. What it does mean is ensuring we select age-appropriate and high-quality material, and provide scaffolding so pupils can understand and therefore enjoy it. Growing to appreciate great children's literature will prime them for the study of complex texts later in life.

For example, exposure to *The Tale of Peter Rabbit*, or *The Lion, The Witch and The Wardrobe* will introduce pupils to the language of the past. Books like *Holes* and *Tom's Midnight Garden* will enable them to encounter complex time sequencing. *Wonder* and *A Series of Unfortunate Events* provide effective introductions to complex narration.

In addition to this, you will want to consider whether you have provided a good balance of genres and text types across the curriculum. Alongside novels, pupils should experience poems, short stories, plays, essays and articles.

Considering all this, you may like to develop or change your reading suggestions by specifying some texts along with clear rationales for them. You could bring colleagues with you by sharing the goals for the reading curriculum and inviting them to make suggestions or join a focus group to review your current offering over time.

In practice: text selections

A plan specifying what texts pupils will read in an example English curriculum could look like the example in the following table. It does not include the non-fiction reading pupils will experience in other areas of the curriculum.

Consider how the texts you recognise may or may not meet the sets of suggested criteria above. You may also want to consider how you could improve on this selection or adapt it to your own context.

	AUTUMN 1	AUTUMN 2	SPRING 1	SPRING 2	SUMMER 1	SUMMER 2
EYFS Reading	• *We're going on a Bear Hunt* by Michael Rosen • *Little Red Hen* by Mary Mapes Dodge	• *Rosie's Walk* by Pat Hutchins • *Owl Babies* by Martin Waddell • *Whatever Next* by Jill Murphy • *Oliver's Vegetables* by Alison Barlett and Vivian French • *The Nativity*	• *What the Ladybird Heard* by Julia Donaldson • *Elmer* by David McKee • *Gingerbread Man* • *Biscuit Bear* by Mini Grey	• *Aliens in Underpants Save the World* by Claire Freedman • *Handa's Surprise* by Eileen Browne • *Goldilocks* • *Three Little Pigs*	• *Giraffes Can't Dance* by Giles Andreae • *Lifecyle of a Chick* • *The Hare and the Tortoise* • *Jack and the Beanstalk*	• *The Rainbow Fish* by Marcus Pfister • *Tiddler* by Julia Donaldson • *Supertato* by Sue Hendra • *Three Billy Goats Gruff* • *Little Red Riding Hood*
EYFS Poetry	• *Incy Wincy Spider* • *Humpty Dumpty*	• *Hickory Dickory Dock* • *Twinkle Twinkle Little Star*	• *Hey, Diddle Diddle* • *Teddy Bear, Teddy Bear*	• *I'm a Little Teapot* • *Baa Baa Black Sheep*	• *Jack and Jill* • *Animal Chatter*	• *The Grand Old Duke of York* • *Dingle, Dangle Scarecrow*
Year 1 Reading	• *The Jolly Postman* by Allan Ahlberg • *Goldilocks*	• *The Ugly Duckling* by Hans Christian Andersen	• *Lost and Found* by Oliver Jeffers • *Traction Man Is Here* by Mini Grey	• *Wanted: The Perfect Pet* by Fiona Robertson • *Beegu* by Alexis Deacon	• *The Lion Inside* by Rachel Bright • *The Tiger who Came to Tea* by Judith Kerr	• *Amazing Grace* by Mary Hoffman

Curriculum design

How to Lead It: Primary English

	AUTUMN 1	AUTUMN 2	SPRING 1	SPRING 2	SUMMER 1	SUMMER 2
Year 1 Poetry	*There Was an Old Man of Peru* by Edward Lear	*Cats Sleep Anywhere* by Eleanor Farjeon	*Dinosaur Rap* by John Foster	*The Ning Nang Nong* by Spike Milligan	*Spaghetti! Spaghetti!* by Jack Prelutsky	*Rhythm of Life* by Michael Rosen
Year 2 Reading	*The Owl who was Afraid of the Dark* by Jill Tomlinson	*Flat Stanley* by Jeff Brown	*A Bear Called Paddington* by Michael Bond	*The Tin Forest* by Helen Ward	*Fantastic Mr Fox* by Roald Dahl	*The Wind in the Willows* by Kenneth Grahame
Year 2 Poetry	*The Engine Driver* by Clive Sansom	*Halfway Down* by A. A. Milne	*Voices of Water* by Tony Mitton	*The Months* by Sara Coleridge	*Bed in Summer* by Robert Louis Stevenson	*Daddy Fell into the Pond* by Alfred Noyes
Year 2 Writing Stimulus	*Wild* by Emily Hughes	*The Owl Who Was Afraid of the Dark* by Jill Tomlinson	• *Wanted: The Perfect Pet* by Fiona Robertson • *The Elves and the Shoemaker* by the Brothers Grimm • *Diary of a Wombat* by Jackie French	• *Wanted: The Perfect Pet* by Fiona Robertson • *Lila and the Secret of Rain* by David Conway • *One Day on our Blue Planet: in the Savannah* by Ella Bailey	*The Tunnel* by Anthony Browne	*Fantastic Mr Fox* by Roald Dahl

	AUTUMN 1	AUTUMN 2	SPRING 1	SPRING 2	SUMMER 1	SUMMER 2
Year 3 Reading	• *Esio Trot* by Roald Dahl • *The Velveteen Rabbit* by Margery Williams	*Charlotte's Web* by E. B. White	*The Lion, The Witch and the Wardrobe* by C. S. Lewis	*The Butterfly Lion* by Michael Morpurgo	*Stig of the Dump* by Clive King	*The Iron Man* by Ted Hughes
Year 3 Poetry	*The Sound Collector* by Roger McGough	*My Brother Might be Bigfoot* by Kenn Nesbitt	*The Owl and the Pussycat* by Edward Lear	*Life Doesn't Frighten Me At All* by Maya Angelou	*The Adventures of Isabel* by Ogden Nash	*Walking with my Iguana* by Brian Moses
Year 3 Writing Stimulus	Myths and legends	*Esio Trot* by Roald Dahl	*Charlotte's Web* by E. B. White	*The Lion, The Witch and the Wardrobe* by C. S. Lewis	*The Butterfly Lion* by Michael Morpurgo	*Stig of the Dump* by Clive King
Year 4 Reading	*The Firework Maker's Daughter* by Philip Pullman	*The Legend of Podkin One-Ear* by Kieran Larwood	*The Nowhere Emporium* by Ross MacKenzie	*Monster Slayer: A Beowulf Tale* by Brian Patten	*The Miraculous Journey of Edward Tulane* by Kate DiCamillo	*Cloud Busting* by Malorie Blackman
Year 4 Poetry	*The King's Breakfast* by A. A. Milne	*Mr Nobody* (Anon)	*From a Railway Carriage* by Robert Louis Stevenson	*A Poem to be Spoken Silently* by Pie Corbett	*Macavity the Mystery Cat* by T. S. Eliot	'A is for Anger' from *An Emotional Menagerie* by The School of Life
Year 4 Writing Stimulus	*Escape from Pompeii* by Christina Balit	*The Firework Maker's Daughter* by Philip Pullman	*The Legend of Podkin One-Ear* by Kieran Larwood	*The Nowhere Emporium* by Ross MacKenzie	*Monster Slayer: A Beowulf Tale* by Brian Patten	*The Miraculous Journey of Edward Tulane* by Kate DiCamillo

Curriculum design

How to Lead It: Primary English

	AUTUMN 1	AUTUMN 2	SPRING 1	SPRING 2	SUMMER 1	SUMMER 2
Year 5 Reading	*The Jungle Book* by Rudyard Kipling	*Brightstorm* by Vashti Hardy	*Goodnight Mr Tom* by Michelle Magorian	*The Explorer* by Katherine Rundell	*Street Child* by Berlie Doherty	*Can You See Me?* by Libby Scott & Rebecca Westcott
Year 5 Poetry	*Whispering Waves* by Edel T. Copeland	*The River* by Valerie Bloom	*It Couldn't Be Done* by Edgar Albert Guest	*Storm in a Rainforest* by Sally Garland	*The Highwayman* by Alfred Noyes	*The British* by Benjamin Zephaniah
Year 5 Writing Stimulus	*Silent Music* by James Rumford	*The Jungle Book* by Rudyard Kipling	*Brightstorm* by Vashti Hardy	*Goodnight Mr Tom* by Michelle Magorian	*The Explorer* by Katherine Rundell	*Street Child* by Berlie Doherty
Year 6 Reading	*The Hobbit* by J. R. R. Tolkien	*The Graveyard Book* by Neil Gaiman	*No Ballet Shoes in Syria* by Catherine Bruton	*Macbeth* by William Shakespeare	*Wonder* by R. J Palacio	*Rooftoppers* by Katherine Rundell
Year 6 Poetry	*The Tyger* by William Blake	*In Flanders Field* by John McCrae	*Night Mail* by W. H. Auden	*Song of the Witches* by William Shakespeare	*If* by Rudyard Kipling	*I Wandered Lonely as a Cloud* by William Wordsworth
Year 6 Writing Stimulus	*The Hound of the Baskervilles* by Arthur Conan Doyle	*The Hobbit* by J.R.R. Tolkien	*The Graveyard Book* by Neil Gaiman	*No Ballet Shoes in Syria* by Catherine Bruton	*Macbeth* by William Shakespeare	*Wonder* by R. J. Palacio

Curriculum planning in a school with mixed-aged classes

If your school includes classes with pupils of mixed ages, you will need to consider this within your curriculum planning. In the National Curriculum for English, the programmes of study are set out by year; however, you are required to cover the programme of study only by the end of a key stage (DfE, 2013, p. 16). If your year groups are combined within a phase, a focus on key-stage expectations will support your planning. Do not forget that you are, however, required to set out and publish your curriculum for English on a year-by-year basis.

A key consideration for mixed-age classes is to have a model of progression to work from. You may find it useful to draw on the ideas in Chapter 3, where we conceptualised progress in three parts: learning more component knowledge, progressively reading and writing more complex texts, and moving from shallow knowledge to deep understanding. Mixed-age teaching is well suited to providing the multiple examples and deliberate practice needed for deepening understanding. You can introduce pupils to content early, and continue to reinforce their knowledge of it over the programme. This will provide pupils with plenty of opportunities to benefit from overlearning (the process of practising beyond proficiency), which can lead to enhanced retention and improved performance.

You will need to sequence the components of teaching over a rolling programme, working backwards from your end goals. In Chapter 5, on assessment, we consider the usefulness of curriculum-related expectations rather than age-related expectations, which could be a useful approach for you to take in deciding what should be achieved by each teaching group. If there are goals specific to a particular year group, you will need to highlight these for teachers on the curriculum overviews. Encouraging teachers to take advantage of flexible groupings will be helpful, as will identifying pupils who might benefit from pre-learning or catch-up activities.

Mixed-age teaching does require skill – but, given young children develop at different paces, so does all teaching. Excellent formative assessment practice will support teachers to teach with precision, identify gaps and misconceptions and adjust the pace of teaching as appropriate. (You will find more support on this in Chapter 5.) Teachers should be aware of the significant variation in the quantity of information young children can hold in their working memory.

Doing all they can to reduce cognitive load as well as considering children's concentration spans will help all learning in a mixed-age classroom.

If you are mixing beyond two year groups, text choice will need careful consideration. You will want to consider the pitch of challenge, but this is often easily overcome with scaffolding, explanations and great storytelling. What possibly requires further thought, if reading is done in broadly mixed age groups, is the content of texts and how age-appropriate they are. Some excellent children's books feature dark or troubling content. While these may pose no problems when introduced at the right point, we should be sensitive to content that may be upsetting for younger pupils.

Conversely, you don't want older pupils to miss out on books as a result of being in a mixed-age classroom. Having class novels that are read together for pleasure rather than for English lessons could be a way to get around this problem. If additional adults are available, you could split the class between you and run daily book groups.

Tips for subject leaders: creating your curriculum

You could draw on the following ideas when creating your curriculum.

- Develop a rolling programme and work backwards from clearly defined end goals. Use the National Curriculum's key-stage expectations to support you.
- Identify the component knowledge pupils will learn as they progress towards these goals.
- Ensure teachers are aware of the curriculum-related expectations they are to cover, and highlight any age-related expectations that need to be secured.
- Develop teachers' use of formative assessment and responsive teaching. Take advantage of flexible groupings to offer pre-learning and keep-up sessions.
- Ensure teachers are aware of the limitations of working memory and are equipped to plan with this consideration in mind.
- Check text choices for any content that may be too disturbing for younger readers.

Ensuring everyone understands the curriculum

A key part of your role involves enabling teachers to implement and enact the curriculum with confidence. You will need to work closely with senior leaders if you are to ensure teachers have adequate resources – including that most precious of resources, time – to deliver the curriculum vision effectively.

You will also need to spend time with your colleagues: time to articulate and collaborate on the school's vision for English, and time to draw on their expertise in understanding pupils' barriers to learning. To teach effectively, teachers need to understand how knowledge builds across the whole school curriculum; they need a sense of what has come before, and what will come afterwards.

Professional development sessions that focus on the English curriculum, that enable you to share documentation and that provide opportunities for collaboration and co-planning are all worthwhile. You may also need to ensure that teachers and teaching assistants are released for subject-specific training so that they can fulfil their roles effectively.

To build regular professional-development provisions into the calendar, a good starting point is to map out what you think you need to achieve and present your plans to the senior leadership team. They will need to consider competing priorities, but starting from a well-planned position should enable you to articulate your case clearly. We will cover how you may go about this in more detail in Chapter 13.

Chapter summary

- You need to consider curriculum intent: what you want pupils to learn and encounter. You then need to sequence this knowledge in a way that enables pupils to make progress.
- Your curriculum should incorporate ways to develop all types of knowledge: declarative, procedural, disciplinary and substantive.
- Choosing appropriate texts is essential. A variety of challenging, diverse and high-quality books can foster literacy, cultural knowledge and readiness for complex texts in secondary education.
- For mixed-age classes, teachers should plan using a rolling programme, set clear goals, sequence component knowledge and select age-appropriate

texts. They should remain responsive to individual learning needs and development stages.
- You should set aside time to guide teachers in understanding the curriculum's aims.

Questions for reflection

- How confident am I in my knowledge of English as a subject? Do I have a clear sense of what makes it distinctive from other subjects taught at primary school? Do I have a vision for what I want pupils to achieve in order to be successful at secondary school?
- How clearly are the components of English mapped out in our curriculum? Is there a shared understanding amongst staff of the curricular goals we want pupils to achieve? Do they understand how teaching in their year group builds on prior learning and primes pupils for future learning? If not, how could I bring staff together to develop understanding of the big picture and how it all fits together?
- How happy am I with the books, novels, rhymes, poems and plays pupils encounter at our school? Do pupils have access to consistently high-quality material? Do all staff understand the rationale for the text choices and the contributions they make to the English curriculum? If not, what steps do I need to take to make improvements?

Explore further

- *Shakespeare and Creative Education* by Daisy Christodoulou (which explores the role of declarative knowledge in creativity): https://daisychristodoulou.com/2017/03/shakespeare-and-creative-education/
- Clare Sealy's blogs about primary-level curriculum planning: https://primarytimery.com

5 Assessment

> As subject leaders, is it important that we are able to measure how effectively the curriculum is delivering on stated learning goals. Once you have a clear sense of curriculum content, you can consider how best to assess it. This chapter deals with that process and will cover:
>
> - understanding assessment, and exploring some helpful assessment-related language, concepts and models
> - putting Assessment for Learning (AfL) and responsive teaching to use in the classroom
> - understanding different elements of summative assessments, and utilising them effectively.
>
> Before you read on, it is worth us flagging that a good understanding of assessment rests on a good knowledge of curriculum. Therefore, whilst you may be dipping in and out of this book, we feel this chapter will make most sense if you first read Chapters 3 and 4, on progression and curriculum planning respectively.

Understanding assessment

Because we can't see what is actually happening in pupils' heads, learning is invisible. I can teach a lesson focused on using full stops accurately – but, unless I then check whether individual pupils can use full stops accurately, I will not know whether they learned anything related to my intentions.

Assessment, then, is an important way to measure the impact of teaching. However, even the most well designed assessments are limited in what they can tell us.

The following example suggests how a teacher may not appreciate how limited her assessment was.

> **Case study: relying on limited assessments**
>
> Sonia is new to teaching. She teaches a lesson on full stops and, at the end of the lesson, all pupils successfully complete a task that demonstrates they can all use full stops effectively. Sonia is delighted that she could move on from this learning objective so quickly.

Sonia was wise to check pupils' understanding rather than making assumptions about their learning. However, as a more experienced teacher, you will know that Sonia's confidence is misplaced. She has not been teaching long enough to know that pupils often forget what they are taught, or fail to replicate their learning in different contexts.

Assessments enable us to make inferences about pupils' learning, but sometimes what our assessments can tell us is limited. Sonia made an inference based on one snapshot of pupil performance. She could have more faith in her inference if her pupils were able to demonstrate correct use of full stops over time, and in a range of different situations.

As a subject leader, you will want to use assessment as effectively as possible. In order to do so, there are some important concepts to understand. We outline these in the sections below before considering how to apply this knowledge and put assessment to good use.

The domain, the curriculum and the sample

Consider the example above again. I'm sure you'd agree that, even if Sonia were to ascertain secure understanding of full stops, it would be a ridiculous jump for her to claim her that, on this basis, her pupils had mastered all aspects of English.

This is because English is a vast subject: the domain of knowledge that sits within it is huge. At primary school, our curriculums direct us to teach a sub-section of that domain. As pupils progress, the curriculum expands. This makes it more and more difficult to measure everything.

As a result, we have to assess pupils' performance against only a sample from the curriculum. In the example above, Sonia's sample is too small for her to infer that her pupils are good at English as a whole.

Validity

Validity is an assessment concept that describes how justified our results-based inferences are. In the example above, Sonia can't make a valid inference about pupil performance across English because her sample is too small.

How we design assessments can also impact the validity of our inferences. Imagine that three teachers in a year group decide to test understanding of full stops weekly. Teacher A reports that all her pupils get 100% in their test each week. Teacher B's pupils score only 10%. You may make an inference that one group of pupils, or one teacher, is more capable than the other.

You may then compare the tests they are using. For example:

TEACHER A's TEST	Add full stops in the correct places. The first example has been done for you. The boy was hungry. The grass is green Dogs like going for walks
TEACHER B's TEST	Add full stops in the correct places. The first example has been done for you. I went to the park. I played on the swings I saw a big dog I called him Max Max was very friendly I patted him Max wagged his tail I went to get ice cream I got chocolate flavour Mum got vanilla Mum and I sat on a bench I ate my ice cream

Clearly, Teacher A's test is far simpler than Teacher B's. The inferences you made comparing the cohorts' or teachers' competence, therefore, would not be valid.

Reliability

Reliability is the extent to which a test is likely to give the same results in different contexts. Potential sources of a test's unreliability include the sample, the marker and circumstances that impacts pupil's performance (Christodoulou, 2016).

The sample

When we test across a broad domain such as English, we pick tasks that sample pupils' knowledge. Take, for example, the Year 6 SAT in Reading. Texts are selected as the basis for the test, and questions test a sample of pupils' vocabulary and background knowledge. Most teachers consider that the papers are harder in some years than in others (Shearing, 2023). In acknowledgement of this potential unreliability, raw scores are converted to scaled scores, to improve the accuracy of comparisons in performance over time using different papers.

The marker

English often requires we make a judgement based on how well we think pupils have performed tasks such as composition. Such judgements are subjective, and it is very unlikely that ten different markers would assign exactly the same mark to a piece of creative writing. The processes of standardisation and moderation are how we work to mitigate this, and are important for you to consider.

The circumstances

It is inevitable that pupils perform differently depending on when and where they sit the test. If a pupil is hungry, has hay fever, revised the content immediately before the test or is distracted by being in a different room, for example, their performance will be impacted.

Using AfL

AfL is an important aspect of good teaching. Developed by Wiliam and Black, it rests on the concept of teachers using information about pupil learning to adapt and teach accordingly (Black et al., 2004). It has a strong evidence base, and is embedded content in the ITT Core Content Framework and the Early Career Framework. However, AfL has so far failed to impact pupil outcomes at national level (Coe, 2013).

This may be because, to many of us, AfL has become reduced to a number of techniques (Fletcher-Wood, 2018). These include, for example:

- using lollipop sticks to call on pupils randomly
- use of mini-whiteboards
- self-assessment and peer-assessment tasks

- written feedback based on 'what went well' and 'even better if'
- highlighting learning objectives to indicate whether they have been met, partially met or not met.

There is nothing intrinsically right or wrong about any of these techniques. However, more important than using techniques labelled as AfL is understanding AfL's principles.

What is AfL actually for?

Summative assessment is intended to assess what pupils have learned. Contrastingly, the key principles of AfL are to expose weaknesses in pupils' learning and prompt remedial responses in the teacher and/or learner.

The reasons AfL hasn't lived up to its promise are explored in Daisy Christodoulou's *Making Good Progress? The future of Assessment for Learning* (2016). She describes how, in a high-stakes accountability system, assessment becomes a tool for monitoring and tracking quality of education. This can, in turn, disincentivise teachers and schools to use assessment systems that expose pupils' weaknesses in learning.

Furthermore, she explains how schools and teachers often use assessments designed to be summative for formative purposes. In English, for example, this could include setting multiple SAT practice questions, or even whole papers, throughout a given key stage. This can make it very difficult to identify the precise component knowledge pupils need in order to improve their performance.

Decoupling formative and summative assessment

Christodoulou suggests we decouple formative and summative assessment. She reminds us that the aim of learning is to create mental models, but that the activities that may create them don't always mirror the appearance of the final product.

Consider, for example, how these learning activities are related to, but not the same as, the final performance:

- Playing scales on the piano does not sound exactly like playing a concerto.
- Dribbling drills do not look exactly like a game of football.
- Colour mixing does not look like painting a masterpiece.

We have explored the 'components before composites' approach to curriculum planning in Chapters 3 and 4: an initial focus on the skills that build towards a competency, rather than on the end-goal itself. A huge advantage of this approach is that small, component parts can be assessed much more effectively and regularly, leading to more timely, precise and helpful feedback. This includes self-assessment: a pianist can hear whether their scales are correct, an artist can judge for themselves whether they are satisfied with the hues they create, and a footballer can tell from drills how accurate his shot is. All can adjust accordingly.

In practice: assessment of components

A plan for assessment of components within composites could look like the example below.

COMPOSITE PERFORMANCE	EXAMPLE COMPONENT KNOWLEDGE	AfL TASKS
What, ultimately, do we want pupils to be able to do?	What units of knowledge do pupils need to achieve this?	What practices will enable precise, helpful feedback?
Read any book independently	Individual sound–spelling correspondences	• Reading a decodable text that features only the sound–spelling correspondences a pupil has been taught • Completing spelling dictation containing words that feature those correspondences
Produce extended writing	Movement of a pencil in a tripod grip	• Drawing lines • Drawing circles • Drawing triangles
Write a narrative text with a beginning, middle and end	Comparative and superlative adjectives	• Writing simple sentences containing comparative adjectives • Write simple sentences containing superlative adjectives

To consider the component knowledge in different aspects of English in more detail, see Chapters 6–11.

Formative assessment and responsive teaching

Teachers constantly make inferences about pupil learning. They may use confused faces, off-task behaviour, lack of response or muddled answers, for example, to judge how well a lesson is going. Whilst this has its uses, a more intentional approach to in-lesson assessment will strengthen teachers' inferences. It will empower them to respond to confusion or errors as they occur.

Responsive teaching is an approach that intentionally embeds formative assessment into teaching. It involves using regular planned assessment points to make inferences about pupils' learning and inform your next steps (Fletcher-Wood, 2018).

One aspect of responsive teaching involves:

- identifying a clear learning goal
- identifying a task that enables inferences about what pupils have learned related to the goal
- using this information to adapt teaching.

In practice: responsive teaching

Responsive teaching in an English lesson might look like the example below.

KNOWLEDGE TO CHECK	END-OF-LESSON ASSESSMENT TASK	RESPONSES TO ERRORS
Composition using comparative adjectives	Write four simple sentences comparing these two dogs: **Figure 5.1:** A great dane and a chihuahua	• Re-teaching the concept • Providing and discussing more examples and non-examples • Modelling writing sentences containing superlatives • Asking pupils to practise using superlatives

Fletcher-Wood suggests using hinge questions within lessons. These are questions that enable us to check quickly whether pupils have understood an important step in the lesson.

> ### In practice: hinge questions
>
> Use of hinge questions in an English lesson might look like the example below.
> - The teacher reviews necessary prior learning, such as use of attributive, predicative and comparative adjectives.
> - The topic of superlative adjectives is introduced: 'Today, we are going to learn about superlative adjectives. A superlative adjective is used to show the highest degree of something. It compares three or more things.'
> - Examples are provided:
>   - If there are three cars, and the blue car is faster than the other two, we use the superlative adjective 'fastest'. The blue car is the fastest car.
>   - If there are five mountains, and one is higher than all the others, we say it is the highest mountain.
> - Ask a hinge question and display the sample sentences below: 'Which of these sentences uses a superlative adjective?'
>   - This book is better than that one.
>   - She is the tallest girl in the class.
>   - My dog is faster than my cat.
>   - This puzzle is easier than the last one.

Ways teachers can elicit feedback

Teachers should aim to gather feedback from the whole class rather than relying on one or two individuals for an answer. This is because, when we ask individuals, we can make inferences about only *their* learning. We are responsible, however, for the learning of the whole class. We could assume the whole class achieved the same answer, but we would not know this for sure.

Instead of asking individuals, teachers could ask pupils to:

- show their answers on mini-whiteboards
- hold up the number of fingers that correlates to the correct answer
- hold up a coloured counter that correlates to the correct answer.

When using the above techniques, teachers should tell pupils to keep their answers secret, wait for all to indicate they have an answer and count down to the reveal. This should ensure pupils who need a little longer to think are included. It also reduces the risk of pupils being influenced by their peers and switching their answers, or waiting to copy others because they are unsure.

Keeping a record

Because we are human and prone to forget, it is useful for teachers to record the results of formative assessments methodically. This will help them to move forwards with a good awareness of pupil and cohort learning needs.

Accountability can unintentionally disincentivise teachers to collect data that expose weaknesses in learning. However, in this case, these are just the kind of data on which you want teachers to focus. It can therefore be more productive *not* to request that teachers submit formative data for you to measure regularly. The decision can also significantly reduce workload burdens, meaning teachers have more time to focus on designing great teaching and assessment activities. Of course, as subject leader, you will want to know how pupils are doing: an important part of leading English is assuring yourself that pupils have learned the curriculum. This can largely, though, be covered by summative assessment (discussed below).

When it comes to formative assessment, the most useful role you can play as subject leader is to support your teachers to set clear learning goals, and to monitor pupils' achievement against those. Holding conversations and professional development sessions that focus on this will have more positive impact on your pupils than a centralised spreadsheet ever could.

Monitoring the link between what has been taught and what has been learned is difficult for one teacher to do in isolation, so a collaborative approach that develops collective expertise is often necessary (Robinson, 2013). Your role in supporting this will be even more important in small or mixed-year-group schools, where it presents particular challenge.

Research has found that teachers in high-achieving schools are more likely to turn to leaders for advice regarding their teaching (Robinson, 2011). If teachers share with you that formative assessment suggests pupils are struggling with an aspect of the curriculum, you should be delighted that they view you as a source of support! This is an opportunity for you to work together to review teaching activities that may better support learning.

Summative assessment

Summative assessment serves a different purpose: it is intended to check learning against a standard or benchmark at the end of an instructional period. It aims to help us understand how a pupil, a cohort or a school is doing.

In *Making Good Progress? The future of assessment for learning* (2016), Christodoulou identifies the features of effective summative assessment. These are summarised below, along with our commentary and considerations for you as the English subject lead.

FEATURE	COMMENTARY	CONSIDERATIONS
Assessments sample from a large domain	<ul><li>It is hard to assess all aspects of the curriculum, so we have to be selective.</li><li>Subject leaders should ensure they select content based on what pupils have been taught and should have learned.</li></ul>	<ul><li>Do your current assessments sample from your taught curriculum?</li><li>Do you have a good sense of what you want to sample in each year?</li><li>Have these assessments been mapped out in advance?</li><li>How valid do you feel inferences based on this sample could be?</li></ul>
Assessments are infrequent	<ul><li>Progress takes time, so summative assessments need to be spaced far enough apart for pupils to have a chance to make progress.</li><li>Assessing too frequently eats into teaching time, and can also demoralise both teachers and pupils.</li></ul>	<ul><li>How many times a year do you hold summative assessments?</li><li>Does this provide enough time for pupils to learn and make progress through the curriculum?</li><li>Do teachers, pupils and parents and carers value these assessments, or are they becoming demoralising?</li></ul>

FEATURE	COMMENTARY	CONSIDERATIONS
Assessments are held under consistent conditions	If we want to compare fairly, we need to be confident the conditions in which assessments are completed are fair.	• Do the assessment tasks change each year, so teachers don't inadvertently 'teach to the test'? • Do all pupils sit the assessments with equal levels of support and guidance? • Do additional adults working with the class, with small groups or one to one know how much support they can provide?
Assessments use standardised scores	Standardised scores enable us to compare results across different assessments, including across years.	• In addition to SAT papers, do you use standardised assessments that generate standardised scores in your school?

Approaches to summative assessment

Teacher assessment

Many primary schools ask teachers to make summative judgments about pupils' attainment standards at the end of each year. These are most usually communicated as whether pupils are working towards, at or above the expected standard.

Schools use different practices to generate these judgements. They may involve teachers setting specific end-of-year tasks, or drawing on a range of information from across the year to reach conclusions.

It is important for you, as subject leader, to think carefully about over-reliance on teacher assessment in English. Evidence consistently demonstrates that this is biased against pupils in ethnic minorities, with SEN, with behavioural problems and from lower socio-economic backgrounds (Christodoulou, 2016). Judgements of pupils' competence in English are particularly subjective, and therefore more vulnerable to such bias. This is not a criticism; it is simply a statement of fact. To deny it would only serve to reinforce such prejudice.

Relying on teacher assessment can also lead to false confidence as pupils progress through school. Most teachers genuinely care about their pupils. They usually have a sense of which pupils sit on the cusp of what they believe to be the expected standard. When it comes to making a judgement the majority of teachers will give these pupils the benefit of the doubt and assess them as working at the expected standard.

If the same pupils had sat a standardised assessment, many of their results would have been just below standard. As a consequence, at cohort level, the cut-off between working at or towards that standard, combined with teacher assessment, risks hiding the fact that some pupils are not progressing through the curriculum as hoped.

A productive alternative may be an approach to summative assessment that draws on teachers assessing a sample of the taught curriculum and combines this with standardised assessment.

Curriculum-related expectations

Didau suggests the use of curriculum-related expectations rather than age-related expectations. This involves having a clear and specific sense of what we expect pupils to have learned within our curriculum, and generating assessments that will sample this knowledge (Didau et al., 2024).

In practice: using a curriculum-related approach

A curriculum-related approach to summative assessment could look like the example below.

- The subject leader provides end-of-year assessments that sample from the growing domain of English (such as phonics or spelling tests). These would be sharply focused on knowledge specified within curriculum plans.
- New tests are generated each year and are not shared with teachers in advance. This frees them to focus on teaching and formatively assessing the entire curriculum rather than a sample.
- The tests are marked and a percentage is generated as a result.
- A percentage of 75%, for example, communicates to school leaders, pupils and parents and carers an inference that the pupil has remembered around 75% of what the curriculum has, so far, set out to teach them.

This approach can help you to gauge to what extent your pupils have learned what you intended. Such assessments can't, however, tell you how well your pupils are doing compared to pupils in other schools. They additionally can't reveal whether subjective judgements could still be prone to teacher bias. Using standardised benchmarking assessments alongside them can help you to navigate this, and to judge to what extent your curriculum is effective.

Standardised benchmarking assessments

Schools can buy external English assessments that convert raw marks into standardised scores. Having sat a test, pupils will be allocated a standardised score between 60 and 140, with 100 being the average. The conversion enables you to benchmark the performance of your pupils against a national cohort, and to compare performance over time. For example, a pupil who achieves a standardised score of 100 on the assessment in one year is doing about as well as a one with the same score for a different assessment the previous year.

It is important to communicate carefully what standardised scores mean. It is common to convert the scores to a statement of standards:

- 60–89: working towards the expected standard
- 90–109: the expected standard
- 110–140: working above the expected standard.

It's worth noting that this system is flawed. Two pupils with standardised scores of 89 and 90 get completely different judgements, despite a difference of only one in their scores; two pupils achieving 90 and 109 get the same judgement, despite a difference of 19. Sharing pupils' actual standardised scores, and helping teachers to understand how standardised scores work, could be a productive approach.

Summative assessment: reading

Like reading itself, the assessment of reading requires a multi-strand approach. The following assessment types used in combination can indicate how effectively the reading curriculum is working for pupils:

- **Phonics assessments** can help us to identify what areas of the code are secure or still need to be learned, and which pupils require additional support. Assessments that assess pupils' ability to hear, manipulate and blend sounds, and segment and decode words will help us to pinpoint the specific difficulties pupils are facing. A good phonics scheme will include assessment tools; we recommend continuing to assess and respond to pupils' phonics competence (decoding and encoding) throughout their time in primary school.

- **Fluency assessments** can tell us how accurately pupils can read at a good pace and enable us to identify which pupils need more support and practice with their reading. Pupils' fluency is assessed by calculating the number of words from a short section of text they can accurately read aloud per minute.

- **Standardised comprehension assessments**, which are commercially available, are very broad and can offer only an overview. They can allow us to track school-wide trends, benchmark pupils and provide useful information to share with parents and carers.

Summative assessment: writing

Comparative judgement is a useful method for assessing pupils' writing. It relies on making comparisons between pupils' work, rather than attempting to use set criteria or a rubric to judge work in isolation. Two pieces of work are presented side by side, with the evaluator simply selecting the piece they think is better each time. Over multiple comparisons, made by multiple judges, a rank order emerges.

This ranking is more reliable than using rubrics or frameworks. The pieces are presented as anonymous, which avoids teacher bias in decisions. The process is also far quicker than traditional marking of extended writing, which is a driver of workload for teachers. All teachers and leaders across the school could act as judges, giving you a strong insight into cohort-wide strengths and weaknesses. This additionally helps teachers to understand standards in classrooms and year groups other than their own. It is possible to complete the process online, using a website such as *No More Marking* to create a free account and upload pupils' work.

Chapter summary

- Assessments enable us to make inferences about pupil learning, but we cannot reach entirely secure conclusions because learning is invisible.

- You should aim to base your assessment systems on reliability, to help you to make more valid inferences.
- You can help teachers make better use of AfL by decoupling formative and summative assessments. The activities you use for each are likely to look very different.
- You can use teacher assessment to focus on whether the taught curriculum has been learned, but need to be aware of teacher bias.
- Summative assessments, including standardised assessments, can help you to understand how effective your curriculum is.

Questions for reflection

- Based on the content of this chapter, how effectively do I think our teachers use formative assessment and responsive teaching? If I don't know, how could I find out?
- Where I feel assessment practice is weak, to what extent do I think the root of this could lie in poor understanding of curriculum goals? What could I do to remedy this?
- How confident am I that our summative assessment system is effective? What changes could I make? How could I go about this?
- How do I know whether pupils in Year 3, for example, are doing well compared to a national cohort?

Example PD session: responsive teaching

You could conduct a PD session on responsive teaching as follows.

As teachers become more confident in teaching responsively, you can adapt these sessions to explore further improvements to the quality of assessment activities. For example, you could develop multiple-choice questions with plausible distractors to help tease out precise misconceptions in pupils' understanding.

TIMING SUGGESTION	SESSION GUIDANCE
Before the session	Ask teachers to bring their lesson plans for the following day.
5 mins	• Describe responsive teaching, drawing on the information in this chapter. • Outline the rationale for the approach, and how it benefits pupils and teachers.
10 mins	• Discuss some examples of precise learning goals and end-of-lesson assessment tasks. • Break down the examples, exploring why they may or may not be effective assessment activities.
2 mins	• Provide an example of a specific learning goal from the English curriculum, and a range of potential assessment tasks. • Ask: 'Which is the best assessment task related to the learning goal?' • Spend more time here if necessary, addressing any misconceptions.

25 mins	• Prompt teachers to review their lesson plans, asking themselves:
	  • Is my learning goal precise?
	  • What assessment activity can I set, to help me understand how well pupils have learned what I intended?
	• Allow time for teachers to write their assessment tasks. Invite them to discuss these in table groups, while you circulate to offer support.

15 mins	• Ask teachers to divide into pairs and to practise setting their assessment tasks for each other. • Ask teachers to review how effectively they feel their partners' tasks would assess the learning goal identified.
After the session	Adapt this template to run a session on hinge questions.

Explore further

- *Making Good Progress? The future of assessment for learning* (2016) by Daisy Christodoulou
- *Responsive Teaching: Cognitive Science and Formative Assessment in Practice* (2018) by Harry Fletcher-Wood
- 'Section 3: Impact. Assessing the curriculum' in *Bringing the English Curriculum to Life* (2024) by David Didau
- *Measuring Up: What Educational Testing Really Tells Us* (2008) by Daniel Koretz
- The EEF's *Shining a spotlight on reading fluency* (2021) blog: https://educationendowmentfoundation.org.uk/news/eef-blog-shining-a-spotlight-on-reading-fluency

6 Teaching early reading

Teaching children to read is probably the most important thing we do at primary school and, as English leads, it is our job to ensure that all teachers have the necessary subject knowledge to do this well. Early reading is the most-researched area in education, and it is incredibly complex. Having said that, in this chapter, we will break down the components into manageable chunks to demystify the process.

In this chapter, we will:

- briefly explore how the development of our writing system impacts the way we teach reading
- look at the 'Simple View of Reading'
- consider the importance of listening comprehension
- begin to look at the 'Rope Model' and its strands for early reading
- explore how to support pupils who need longer to internalise phonics
- review the evidence bases for fluency practice and vocabulary instruction, and how these look in EYFS and Key Stage 1
- explore the barriers some pupils face when learning to read, and some practical approaches to overcoming them
- reflect on the purpose and importance of the Phonics Screening Check and our role in supporting colleagues.

A brief history of writing and how it impacts reading

It is vital for us to understand the elements required to get pupils to the point of reading and comprehending a text independently. In order to do so, we need to track back to how writing developed.

Reading is inextricably linked to writing; we read what has been written down. That may seem obvious, but unpicking this connection helps us to understand both skills, and to identify our best bets for teaching early reading.

Early writing

The earliest evidence for writing dates to about 5,300 years ago. At this time, people used logographs – symbols – to represent whole words (Robinson, 2007). As our desire to communicate thoughts and ideas in writing became more complex, the symbols evolved. Modern writing systems now use symbols to represent sounds within words.

Writing today

In some languages, such as Japanese, the symbols represent whole syllables. This is possible because there are only around 100 syllables in spoken Japanese. However, in English, there are approximately 15,000.

As a result, written English uses letters or groups of letters (graphemes) to represent the smallest units of sound (phonemes) within words. Every word in English is formed from a combination of just 44 phonemes. Once we learn the sound-to-spelling correspondences for all 44, we can decode and read any written word.

This sounds straightforward, but there are further complications. Perfetti, for example, asserts that English is a morphophonemic language (Perfetti & Verhoeven, 2011). In other words, the letters represent sounds *and* hold meaning. This makes the code more complex. We discuss the impact of this in Chapter 8.

Another factor to consider is the number of homophones in the English language: 'their', 'there', and 'they're', for example. There are, additionally, 200 spellings to represent our 44 sounds – so one sound can be represented by more than one letter, and one letter can represent more than one sound. For example, the sound /ər/ is spelt differently in 'curt', 'worm', 'squirmed', 'fern' and 'heard', and the letter 'o' represents different sounds in 'dog', 'go' and 'do'.

The sound unit used in a writing system must match the spoken word (Castles et al., 2018). The principle that there is a systematic relationship between phonemes and graphemes in languages with alphabets is called the 'alphabetic principle' (Such, 2021). Teaching pupils these relationships through phonics is, therefore, a crucial component of reading instruction. We can also apply code knowledge to teach spelling (see Chapter 10).

Mismatches between written and spoken words

Where the sound unit in a writing system does not appear to match a spoken word, this is likely to be for one of the three following reasons.

- The reader has not been taught the particular sound-to-spelling correspondence. For example, a reader may not have been taught that the letters 'ey' can represent the sound /eɪ/ in 'they', 'grey', 'obey', 'prey' etc.
- The pronunciation of the word has changed over time. For example, studying the etymology of the word 'knight' teaches us that in Old and Middle English the /k/ was voiced. However, by about 1750, the /k/ was no longer voiced. In sister languages, such as German, the /k/ is still pronounced in 'kn' spellings.
- The word comes from another language and has been adopted, for example 'ballet' (from French) in which 'et' is pronounced /eɪ/, or 'photograph' (from Greek), in which 'ph' is pronounced /f/.

The 'Simple View of Reading'

To help us make sense of the components required to teach children to read, we can look at the 'Simple View of Reading'. This model was introduced by three researchers: Gough, Hoover and Tunmer, in the late 1980s and early 1990s.

The Simple View of Reading has often been presented as a linear model, suggesting decoding comes first and language comprehension afterwards (Catts, 2018). However, Hoover, Gough and Tunmer represented reading comprehension as the *combination* of decoding and comprehension of language, resulting in reading for meaning. They wrote it as a multiplication problem:

Deoding (D) × Language Comprehension (LC) = Reading Comprehension (RC)

We know that, when we multiply anything by zero, the outcome is zero. Therefore, if either word recognition or language comprehension is missing, children will not understand what they are reading.

At the early stages of learning to read, we want to manage pupils' cognitive load. We can do this by focusing on learning the phonic code so well that pupils can decode automatically. This helps them to experience success as they realise the squiggles on the page represent words with which they are familiar. Being able to read words quickly then frees up working memory to focus on comprehending what text means. By emphasising decoding practice in EYFS and Year 1, therefore, we can help pupils to comprehend more-complicated texts later on.

Just focusing on learning the phonic code is not enough, though. We also need to remember the language comprehension factor of the Simple View of Reading. By reading and discussing lots of stories and poems with rich vocabulary, we can build pupils' language comprehension. We will discuss this more, later in the chapter.

As pupils learn to read, they may focus more on one element than another at different points. We should remember, though, that both elements are necessary for reading.

Language comprehension

While they're in the early stages of learning to read, we can develop pupils' language comprehension by building their vocabulary and background knowledge. We do this by reading and sharing lots of high-quality texts with them. This will develop their understanding of story structures and text types, as well as syntax.

Listening comprehension

It is important that we understand the difference between listening comprehension (practised while texts are heard) and language comprehension (practised when pupils are reading texts themselves).

Research evidence suggests a close correlation between listening comprehension, which is already well established before most children start school, and language comprehension. Listening comprehension relates to speech, during which the speaker uses their voice to indicate tone and pace. In language comprehension, the reader relies on syntax, punctuation and vocabulary to build meaning. Written language tends to be more formal, with more complex syntax.

It is, therefore, vital that pupils have a wide range of fiction and non-fiction *read to* them. This is not directly developing language comprehension, because pupils are not using the syntax and punctuation on the page to build meaning. However, the person reading aloud is building the pupils' vocabulary and knowledge of texts.

Text selection for daily 'story time'

When you're planning time for pupils to hear texts read aloud, we suggest thinking carefully about the opportunity-to-cost ratio. We have a limited amount of time with pupils in EYFS and Key Stage 1, and we cannot introduce them to even a fraction of the wonderful literature available. We therefore need to plan ahead and have a clear rationale for which texts we are going to introduce to pupils – while still allowing time for pupils to request their favourites. (In Chapter 4, we consider criteria for text selection and share an example reading canon.)

As English lead, you may like to consider how you can ensure teachers are reading rich fiction and non-fiction texts to pupils every day. It may be timetabled, but is it happening consistently? Which texts are being read? Is a good range of texts chosen, or do teachers read only texts suggested by the pupils or from their own repertoire? Do teachers feel confident reading aloud? Are they reading with expression?

The 'Reading Rope' model

We've seen that it's not enough for pupils only to be able to read words on the page: they also need to understand what the words mean, and how they connect to make meaningful phrases, sentences and paragraphs. How do we ensure this, though?

The Simple View of Reading has been further broken down by Dr Hollis Scarborough (2001). In her Reading Rope model, she identifies five strands within the language comprehension element of reading. She incorporates decoding in the element of word recognition, including phonological awareness and sight recognition alongside it.

ELEMENT	STRAND
Language comprehension	Background knowledge
	Vocabulary
	Language structures
	Verbal reasoning
	Literacy knowledge
Word recognition	Phonological awareness
	Decoding
	Sight recognition

Fluency

Both Scarborough and Hoover, Gough and Tunmer identify that reading-fluency practice combines all elements. Fluent reading is the accurate reading of a text at a conversational pace, with appropriate expression. It requires accuracy, automaticity and prosody (understanding of intonation and rhythm patterns). Fluency doesn't develop overnight, but rather progressively over time; it requires a lot of practice.

Implications for teaching early reading

In EYFS and Year 1, the majority of reading lessons will be spent learning the phonic code. Using a phonics programme that has been developed by experts will ensure the code is introduced in a rigorous and systematic sequence. You will want to ensure that implementation of your phonics programme provides plentiful opportunities for new knowledge to be practised and revisited until pupils can apply it automatically.

During daily story time, teachers can build the language-comprehension elements of vocabulary and background knowledge by reading a wide range of fiction and non-fiction with pupils. As pupils' code knowledge becomes more proficient, they will be able to read a wider range of texts themselves, and the language-comprehension elements can be developed through those texts.

In practice: elements of a typical phonics lesson

A teacher's approach to a typical phonics lesson could look like the example below:
- The teacher introduces new code knowledge following the order set in the school's chosen phonics programme.
- They review previously taught code knowledge by reading a decodable text. (Some programmes specify revisiting code knowledge taught in the previous unit so that pupils recall learning using the principle of spaced practice (see Chapter 2). Other schemes rely on teachers' professional judgement about which codes to review and when.)
- The teacher uses sentence dictation to apply code knowledge taught in earlier units. (As with reviewing code knowledge, some schemes specify using code knowledge taught from two units earlier, whilst other schemes rely on teachers' professional judgement.)

Routines for phonics lessons

In Chapter 2, we looked at the research evidence for how learning happens (Willingham, 2017). This includes the limits on our working memory and how easily our attention can be disrupted. We know young children find it especially hard to zone out distractions and stay focused. To help mitigate this, it is helpful to support teachers in planning a routine for phonics lessons and to keep it consistent. This helps pupils to focus on code knowledge and reading instead of using valuable working memory to understand new routines or activity instructions. Again, when choosing your phonics scheme, it is worth considering how each scheme supports you with this.

Pupils who need longer to internalise the code

Some pupils will need a little more practice than their peers, which is perfectly normal. A well-structured phonics scheme should help you to tackle this using the three phases outlined in the 'In practice' feature above. Having this structure gives pupils who need more practice time to consolidate their learning because they are revisiting previously taught learning at regular intervals. As English lead, it is important for you to ensure that colleagues understand this, and the importance of persisting with phonics teaching for pupils who need more practice time. You will also need to be vigilant to ensure pupils are not asked to guess words or to learn lists of high-frequency words by sight. This will only lead to problems later and slow down pupils' ability to decode words.

Repeating parts of lessons

If pupils still need more practice, repeating the part of the lesson with which they struggled can have a hugely positive impact. For example, if a pupil struggled to build words with the new code knowledge taught that day, the teacher can reteach word-building later in the day. This kind of investment up front is called 'keep-up intervention'. If timetabled and done rigorously, it can significantly reduce the need for *catch-up* intervention to support pupils who have fallen behind. This not only reduces the work and stress loads on teachers and educational support staff; it also helps pupils feel successful and confident as learners.

It is therefore worth considering how timetables are structured in relation to this. They should enable teachers to repeat part or all of phonics lessons for pupils who struggled to keep up or who were absent from school. The investment is well worth it: you will see your staff and pupils reap the benefits later. Ensuring pupils have time to practise their code knowledge will also strengthen their mental representations. We look at this in more detail in Chapter 9.

In practice: running a keep-up intervention

A keep-up intervention in Year 1 might look like the example below.
- A Year 1 teacher has been introducing alternative spellings for the sound /eɪ/. By the end of the lesson, she notices that two pupils are still saying the individual letters 'a' 'e' in 'make' as /æ/ and /e/. The teacher makes a note of the pupils and the specific sound–spelling correspondence on a daily tracker, ready for a same-day intervention.
- The teacher schedules time for the intervention at the end of the day, organising for a teaching assistant to supervise pupils getting their coats and bags.
- During the intervention, the teacher models the /eɪ/– 'ay' correspondence again, and gives the pupils time to practise reading and writing words from that morning's lesson.
- She makes a note to call on those pupils regularly in the following phonics lessons that week, to ensure they get regular practice.

Fluency practice

There is a rich evidence base for fluency practice and the key role it plays in building reading competency. In 2000, The National Reading Panel identified fluency as one of the 'big five' components for the effective teaching of reading. More recently, The Department for Education (DfE) published *The Reading Framework* (2023), which features a strong focus on building reading fluency at each stage.

What does fluency practice look like in EYFS, Year 1 and beyond?

Fluency practice in EYFS, Year 1 and early Year 2 looks very different from fluency practice later in Year 2 and beyond. In EYFS and Year 1, pupils need plenty of practice building words, and reading and rereading their decodable texts. They need lots of practice blending the letters to turn them into words, as well as manipulating the letters. Playing 'sound swap' games, in which the initial, middle and final letters in CVC words are replaced, are an ideal way to help pupils practice these skills.

As pupils' code knowledge builds and pupils are able to read decodable texts a few pages long, we can begin to extend fluency practice. We can do this by asking pupils to read and reread two or three sentences.

In Chapter 7, we consider how to structure reading-fluency lessons as pupils begin reading to learn rather than learning to read.

In practice: elements of a fluency lesson in EYFS and Year 1

By the middle of EYFS, a fluency lesson may look like the example below.
- The EYFS teacher puts a decodable text under the visualiser, ensuring it is long enough that pupils are reading it and not memorising it.
- She points to the words, and asks individual pupils to read one or two sentences each. At this early stage, their reading is laboured because the pupils are applying their code knowledge.
- The teacher calls on several pupils to read the same section of text, one after another. She asks pupils who need a little more practice to read after they have heard one or two peers read.

- She then asks the whole class to read the text aloud together. This allows them the maximum opportunity to practise their code knowledge with support, gives pupils who need more practice the time to consolidate, and helps her to keep the pupils learning together.

Tips for teachers: maximising reading opportunities for all pupils

You could encourage teachers to draw on the following ideas for maximising reading opportunities.

- Create a culture in which all pupils know they may be called on to read at any point in a phonics lesson. This can be done by calling on pupils seemingly at random to read and reread sections of text. By making your choice of pupil unpredictable, you are increasing the likelihood of all pupils reading along at all times.
- In advance, identify who you will call on. You may decide to call on confident pupils first, to model the process for others, and then on less-confident pupils. This will allow them the opportunity to have followed along and read the section several times in their heads first.
- As you progress through EYFS, pupils will be ready to read from their own copies of the text. At this stage, introduce the concept of a 'reading finger'. Model putting your finger under the word from which you are going to begin reading, and ask the pupils to do the same. Teach pupils to track the text with their reading finger. This will help you to monitor whether they are reading along in their heads as you or their peers read aloud.
- To gauge whether pupils are reading along in their heads, ask individuals to take over the reading quickly: they should be able to do so straight away. You could also introduce a routine in which clicking your fingers indicates everyone should join in. This works well if you click your fingers at the final words in a sentence.

The importance of building vocabulary

In Chapter 2, we explored the evidence base for teaching vocabulary. From the age of five, children acquire most new vocabulary through reading (Beck et al., 2013). However, if they don't have a good vocabulary base to start with, they will struggle to understand what they read. They are less likely to value and enjoy reading. If they don't enjoy reading, they're less likely to be motivated to read and therefore won't continue to acquire the vocabulary needed to engage with all aspects of the curriculum.

Implicit and explicit vocabulary instruction

Traditionally, we have asked pupils to guess the meaning of new words by using context clues from the text. This can be a time-consuming process and often, even after asking three or four pupils what they think the word means, we will have to give a definition. It's much more efficient to start by giving the pupils a picture (if the word is a concrete noun or verb for a familiar activity) or a child-friendly definition. Pupils can then practise using that word in context.

There are two ways to teach vocabulary: implicitly and explicitly. We simply don't have time to teach every word explicitly, so implicit teaching is often preferred.

When teaching implicitly, it may be enough for pupils to learn a new word through exposure in context. This may be a one-off teaching point: for example, 'sofa' is another word for 'settee'. Another way to learn vocabulary implicitly is through frequent, repeated exposure. Reading a word in a clear, directive context may be sufficient. For example, if the word indicates how a character is speaking, you can read their speech in that tone.

Explicit instruction is important for high-leverage vocabulary that is key to understanding a text. For example, if the word 'reluctant' is key to understanding how a main character is feeling, it's a high-leverage word on which it's worth spending time. Including synonyms and antonyms in explanations can help pupils to make links with their existing knowledge. To ensure pupils remember and use these words themselves, it is also important to make time to revisit the words and practise using them across several lessons.

Vocabulary tiers

Beck, McKeown and Kucan (2013) grouped vocabulary into three tiers to help us think about which words should be taught explicitly.

VOCABULARY TIER	EXPLANATION	EXAMPLES
Tier 1	This is basic vocabulary that we often use in speech. We don't usually need to teach these words directly: often, showing a picture or pointing to an object is sufficient.	book, boy, walk, cat, yellow
Tier 2	These are high-frequency, often descriptive words, commonly with more than one meaning. They occur more usually in formal language and in literature.	masterpiece, engaged, benevolent, capacity
Tier 3	These are low-frequency, often subject-specific words. Tier 3 vocabulary should be taught explicitly.	habitat, climate, revolution, occupation, taxonomy

For pupils to be on track for building the vocabulary knowledge required for the curriculum at secondary school, they should learn about 7,000 Tier 2 words at primary school. We can't teach all these words in discrete vocabulary lessons, so we need to have a clear strategy for how we teach vocabulary.

Tips for teachers: choosing which words to teach explicitly

To support staff with vocabulary instruction, you may like to consider a standardised approach to begin with. You could encourage teachers to use the following checklist when choosing which words to teach explicitly.

- Are pupils likely to see or hear the word often in other contexts?
- Will it be useful in pupils' writing?
- Is it related to already familiar words or ideas?
- Is it key to comprehension of a text or topic?

- Does the context provide insufficient information for pupils to infer meaning?

Remember, the best sources for new vocabulary are books that teachers read aloud to pupils.

In practice: teaching vocabulary from EYFS to Year 2

A vocabulary lesson for pupils between EYFS and Year 2 might look like the example below.

- A teacher considers a text that's familiar to the pupils: a story about a dinosaur that doesn't want to go to the dentist. Knowing she shouldn't tax pupils' working memory with more than a few target words, she selects just one: 'reluctant'.
- The teacher prepares a child-friendly explanation of the word: 'If you're reluctant, you are not sure you want to do something.' She identifies a picture in the book in which the dinosaur is hiding under the table.
- When she reaches the page that features the word, the teacher contextualises the word by drawing attention to the picture.
- She reads the sentence in which the word appears, and then repeats the word: 'Tyrannosaurus was reluctant to go to the dentist. He was reluctant.'
- The teacher says, 'Say the word with me. We can use the "my turn, your turn" technique.' This gives pupils time to create a phonological representation of the word.
- The teacher gives her prepared explanation of the word.
- She includes the word in a question about the book – 'Who was reluctant to sit in the dentist's chair?' – and then in examples out of its context. For example:
  - 'I was reluctant to try a new food yesterday because I didn't know if I'd like it.'
  - 'I was reluctant to go on the ride at the theme park because I thought it looked a bit scary.'
  - 'I was reluctant to go for a bike ride after school because it was raining.'
- The teacher relates the word to the pupils' own experience: 'Can you tell me something you might be reluctant to do?'

- She refers back to the word later in the day, the next day and at least once more that week. She continues this spaced practice by including the word in vocabulary sessions at least once the following week, and again two and four weeks later.

Understanding the barriers some pupils face

As we have explored, reading is a complex, hugely interwoven process. It is inevitable that some pupils will struggle with elements of it. In the early stages of learning to read, they tend to fall into two groups: those who need more practice building code knowledge, and those who need to build their vocabulary knowledge. There will also be some pupils who need both.

Dyslexia

Discussing dyslexia presents a conundrum because there is no universally agreed definition of it. However, it is widely agreed that dyslexia can be described as a difficulty in reading words, and it has genetic, neurobiological causes (Snowling & Hulme, 2005).

The vast majority of people who have severe difficulty reading at word level have difficulties with phonological processing in some form (Kilpatrick & O'Brien, 2019). Phonological processing is the ability to analyse and manipulate phonemes. There is no clear delineation between people who are dyslexic and those who struggle with word reading but don't quite meet the threshold. Rather than waiting for a diagnosis of dyslexia (or lack of diagnosis), it is more productive to consider, identify and target pupils' specific phonological difficulties.

Phonological difficulties

The table below is a useful starting point to consider typical phonological difficulties and how they may manifest. Essentially, we want pupils to segment, blend and manipulate sounds in words confidently. Your phonics programme should include assessment materials to support teachers in identifying not just gaps in code knowledge but also weaknesses in blending, segmenting and manipulating the code (Wolf, 2008). We also suggest working with your school's SENCo.

Once you have identified the difficulties, you can focus additional support on them. Using words that contain continuants – sounds you can stretch – is helpful in supporting pupils with phonological difficulties. For example, for the word 'fin', you can stretch out the phonemes as you say the word slowly: /f/ /ɪ/ /n/. This gives a pupil more time to hear and process the sounds. Compare this to the word 'bit'. We can't make the /b/ or /t/ any longer without introducing a schwa, so must process and identify the sounds more quickly. (John Walker's excellent blog *Can't Blend Won't Blend* gives further solutions: see the 'Explore further' section at the end of this chapter.)

TYPE OF PHONOLOGICAL PROCESSING DIFFICULTY	EXPLANATION
Sound isolation	Difficulty recognising individual sounds, such as /b/ at the beginnings of 'bog', 'bid' and 'big'.
Sound discrimination	Difficulty discriminating between individual sounds in words; for example, not being aware of the different vowel sounds in 'sib' and 'seb'
Sound manipulation	Difficulty remembering a simple sequence of sounds
Sound blending	Difficulty blending (some) individual sounds to form a word, or mixing up sounds
Syllable identification	Difficulty hearing and clapping the syllables in words
Rhyme identification	Difficulty identifying or suggesting rhyming words

Phonics for struggling readers beyond Year 1

It can be tempting, when a struggling reader enters Year 2, to decide phonics hasn't worked for them and to encourage them to learn whole words by sight.

However, as we discussed in terms of how our writing system developed, the symbols on the page have all been created to represent the sounds of spoken words. (We unpick this further in Chapter 10, where we explore the history of English.)

Early writing systems used logographs to represent whole words, but they had to evolve because our memories can retain only about 2,000–5,000 of them (Gough & Hillinger, 1980). If we ask pupils to memorise whole words, we are essentially asking them to memorise words as logographs, and we are therefore limiting their ability to read to 2,000–5,000 of them – in comparison to the 7,000 Tier 2 words pupils should learn in primary school alone.

By the time pupils reach the end of Year 1, most phonics schemes will have introduced them to about 65 sound–spelling correspondences. These are the sound–spelling correspondences required for the phonics screening check taken at the end of Year 1 in English schools. However, there are around 200 sound–spelling correspondences in English, 175 of which are common and important to learn. (The remaining 25, such as the /æ/ in meringue (spelled with an 'i'), are used in so few words that we can learn them incidentally.)

Teaching pupils sight words may result in a short-term gain in Year 2, but it will limit their ability to read increasingly complex texts across Key Stage 2. We can ensure long-term success in reading by continuing to teach and practise the phonic code with them.

The phonics screening check (PSC)

As English lead, your ability to support teachers in EYFS and Key Stage 1 relies on you having a good grasp of how pupils learn to read. When the PSC was first introduced, the Standards and Testing Agency stated, 'The purpose of the phonics screening check will be to confirm that all pupils have learned phonic decoding to an age-appropriate standard' (DfE, 2025).

In other words, the check assesses whether a pupil is working at the minimum expected standard of decoding for a six-year-old. It does not assess whether a pupil has mastered the phonic code: it assesses only 60–65 of the 200 sound–spelling correspondences in English. In other words, it is the tip of the iceberg.

The DfE describes the check as a 'light touch' assessment. It is an early screener to check pupils are not going unnoticed and falling through the cracks. Any pupil who is not meeting the standard of the check at the end of Year 1 is highly likely to fall behind in learning to read.

You therefore need to check that strong systems are in place to ensure high-quality phonics instruction, and also that practice is directed for at-risk pupils in EYFS and Key Stage 1. For some pupils, you may need to ensure this support is also in place in Key Stage 2.

Your phonics programme should provide you with a detailed plan that shows which sound–spelling correspondences are taught when, and when they are revisited. This should help you to ensure teachers are systematically monitoring pupils' progress. If teachers are working through the phonics programme at the anticipated pace, you can also easily assess whether pupils are on track at any point in the year. You can then check whether pupils who are not on track are receiving keep-up or catch-up interventions, and monitor the impact of them.

In Chapter 7, we will explore further barriers that pupils may face as they begin reading to learn rather than learning to read.

Case study: supporting teachers to secure code knowledge

Laura, an English lead, reviews pupils' progress in phonics with the EYFS teacher at the end of the autumn term. They identify a group of pupils who are not secure in the code knowledge taught, despite the teacher calling on them to decode words every lesson.

Laura suggests repeating the phonics lesson the same day for those pupils, but the teacher explains she doesn't have an additional adult to support her with this. However, recognising the pupils are starting to fall behind, the class teacher agrees to repeat phonics lessons with the whole class when necessary, directing all her questions towards the pupils who are less secure.

As a result, the pupils who are starting to fall behind catch up quickly. By the end of term, all the pupils in EYFS, apart from one pupil with specific learning needs, are secure in the code knowledge they have been taught.

Chapter summary

- English follows the alphabetic principle, which means spellings have been derived to represent the sounds in words.
- The Simple View of Reading shows that reading comprehension is the result of word recognition combined with language comprehension.
- Reading stories aloud to pupils builds their vocabulary knowledge and develops their linguistic comprehension. In turn, this builds their language comprehension.
- Scarborough's Reading Rope model can suggest constructive structures for teaching early reading.
- A typical phonics lesson will contain three parts: an introduction to new code knowledge, the retrieval of recent previously taught code knowledge and application of code knowledge taught at an earlier date.
- Keep-up interventions have more impact than catch-up interventions.
- Fluency practice helps pupils internalise code knowledge and build reading automaticity.
- Implicit and explicit instruction both have roles in the practice of teaching vocabulary.
- You should continue phonics teaching for struggling readers, rather than resorting to word recognition.
- It can be most productive to identify and target pupils' specific phonological processing difficulties.

Questions for reflection

- How is phonics taught in our school?
- How do phonics lessons link to the wider English curriculum in different year groups?
- Do I feel I have a training or development need in this area?
- When do we teach vocabulary? Is it a key component in reading lessons?
- How intentional is vocabulary teaching across the school? Is there a common approach across EYFS and Key Stage 1?

- How do teachers select the vocabulary to teach, and what forms the basis of their choices?
- How has this chapter supported my understanding of reading as a process, and of the component knowledge that pupils need?
- What do I think the strengths of our current practice are, and where would I like to develop more expertise and competence? How might this impact our future English leadership?

Example PD session: whole-class fluency

You could conduct a PD session on whole-class fluency as follows.

Although the plan refers to fluency lessons in EYFS and Year 1, it is likely that some pupils in all year groups will be working below year-group expectations. This PD task is therefore likely to be useful for all colleagues. You may also like to refer to the 'In practice' fluency intervention section in Chapter 7 to adapt the task for pupils in older year groups, too.

TIMING SUGGESTION	SESSION GUIDANCE
Before the session	Pre-record yourself teaching a short reading-fluency lesson using the prompts in the 'In practice' feature titled 'Elements of a fluency lesson in EYFS and Year 1'. (60 seconds on this should be sufficient.)
10 mins	Use the section of this chapter on fluency practice to explain the features and importance of whole-class fluency.
15 mins	• Share the prompts from the 'In practice' feature, and ask staff to look for them as you play the video clip. • Give staff, in groups of two or three, two minutes to share their observations with each other. • Spend three minutes taking feedback and reinforcing key points as a group. • Model the fluency lesson with the staff participating as pupils. • As a team, answer this question: 'What are the key features of reading-fluency lessons at EYFS and Year 1 in our school?'

TIMING SUGGESTION	SESSION GUIDANCE
10 mins	Ask small groups to practise leading and participating in the same fluency lesson. Rotate roles amongst staff until everyone has had at least one opportunity to lead the lesson.

Explore further

- Linguistic Phonics's blog: https://linguisticphonics.wordpress.com/
- *Early Reading Instruction: What Science Really Tells Us About How to Teach Reading* (2006) by Diane McGuinness
- *The Art and Science of Teaching Primary Reading* (2021) by Christopher Such
- *Primary Reading Simplified* (2025) by Christopher Such
- The Science of Reading's podcast: https://linguisticphonics.wordpress.com/
- The Literacy Blog's *Can't Blend Won't Blend* (2022) by John Walker: https://theliteracyblog.com/2022/08/21/cant-blend-wont-blend-a-reprise

7 Beyond early reading

Once pupils have learned to decode, and have sufficient vocabulary and background knowledge to understand what they are reading, they can use reading to help them learn new information. This is often called the 'reading to learn phase' (Chall ,1983).

To support your oversight of the subject as English lead, it's important for you to know and understand the whole journey to becoming a confident reader. It's also important that everyone teaching reading has a firm understanding of the full journey. It all links together, and every class will undoubtedly include pupils working both behind and ahead of their year group's expected standards.

In this chapter, we will cover:

- how the Reading Rope model can be applied beyond early reading
- the role of background knowledge in forming inference skills and developing 'situation models'
- the importance of developing literacy knowledge
- implicit and explicit vocabulary teaching at Key Stage 2
- planning a sequence of reading lessons
- the importance of reading for pleasure, through both motivation and competency
- ways to address problems with reading fluency and comprehension
- creating a positive reading culture.

The Reading Rope revisited

Scarborough's Reading Rope (2001), as we explored in the previous chapter, can be a valuable model for unpicking the elements required for reading comprehension.

This model can be as helpful for later-stage reading at as it is when pupils are just beginning to read. It can therefore be useful to continue referring to this model when planning and teaching lessons. It helps us to understand precisely what we need to teach, practise and apply with pupils during reading lessons.

The model identifies five strands within language comprehension and three strands within word recognition that are necessary for fully understanding what we read. In the following table, we have listed the strands within each component and given examples of how this may look in practice beyond early reading.

STRAND		IN PRACTICE
LANGUAGE COMPREHENSION	Background knowledge	• Incorporating secondary texts to deepen understanding of primary texts (e.g. reading non-fiction extracts to build knowledge of Victorian workhouses when reading Dickens's *Oliver Twist*) • Developing wider reading at home (e.g. drawing on a range of texts in the class library and engaging with research tasks) • Using non-fiction texts across all curriculum subjects (e.g. sourcing short texts to read aloud in foundation subject lessons) • Using analogies where possible (e.g. linking topics to pupils' existing knowledge and then deepening their understanding of the similarities and differences)
	Vocabulary	• Semantic mapping (e.g. defining, describing and explaining the purpose of the word 'government') • Using the Frayer model (e.g. defining the word 'trust', identifying the concept's key characteristics, and giving examples and non-examples that illustrate it) • Using synonyms, antonyms and collocations (words or phrases that are often used together), which is especially valuable for EAL learners • Changing word classes and tenses, which is especially good for identifying misconceptions, helping to hone understanding and developing apt use of words • Exploring root words, prefixes and suffixes, discussing etymology (the history of words) to assist recall of words' meanings
	Language structures	• Developing the skills of close reading and analysis at sentence level (e.g. noting sentence length and discussing the deliberate choices authors make) • Deconstructing complex sentences and moving clauses (e.g. identifying examples of multiclause sentences and discussing the effect of swapping clause order or using different conjunctions) • Using given sentence parameters for answering questions (e.g. beginning answers with fronted adverbials or including the phrase 'for example')
	Verbal reasoning	• Analysing the meaning of text, its tone and its inferred meaning • Identifying metaphor as a device, or extended metaphor to convey a deeper message • Debating using evidence from a text and stock phrases that structure explanations
	Literacy knowledge	• Considering the author and context of a book • Discussing the significance of a text, and the reasons it was chosen • Making links between authors, genres and/or themes • Exploring the purposes of all texts, both primary and secondary • Expanding wider reading by choosing books with the same authors or themes

STRAND		IN PRACTICE
WORD RECOGNITION	Phonological awareness	• Foregrounding understanding that syllables make up words • Focusing on individual sounds within words
	Decoding	• Practising alphabetic principles and sound–spelling correspondences • Participating in daily phonics sessions • Practising fluency and prosody whenever possible
	Sight recognition	• Instantly processing familiar words • Practising fluency and prosody whenever possible

Vocabulary and background knowledge

When considering the example practices in the table, it is worth thinking about the inter relatedness of vocabulary and background-knowledge strands. There is a strong evidence base that vocabulary and background knowledge are essential for understanding a text (Kintsch, 1988; Hirsch, 2013; Quigley, 2020).

It makes common sense that, if you read a scientific report about the effects of pesticides on pollination, your background knowledge and vocabulary knowledge about plants will help you understand the text. If you don't have a basic understanding of the parts of a plant and different types of pollination, the report will be a challenging read.

Equally, if you were introducing pupils to C. S. Lewis's *The Lion, the Witch and the Wardrobe* and they had not studied World War 2, they would find it confusing that a group of children had gone to live with a stranger in the countryside. Understanding the context and subject-specific vocabulary will help them to understand the story opening better.

Understanding the importance of building vocabulary and background knowledge together will influence how you teach reading lessons. In Chapter 6, we explored the contrast between implicit and explicit vocabulary teaching for early reading. In Key Stage 2, most vocabulary can be taught implicitly during lessons, largely because it is related to more-developed webs of background knowledge. For the same reason, explicit teaching can be achieved fairly simply: if a teacher reads the class text ahead of the lesson, they can identify vocabulary pupils are unlikely to know and prepare child-friendly definitions. Teachers may want to address high-utility words in more detail, and we will unpick how to approach this later in this chapter.

Understanding cognitive load when teaching reading

Looking at the first two Reading Rope strands – background knowledge and vocabulary – we are reminded that we need to hold a lot of information in our memory before we can fully comprehend or understand a text. In the Chapter 2 section on cognitive science, we explored the limited capacity of our working memory: it can hold only a small amount of new information at any one time. This means that building background knowledge and vocabulary in our long-term memory is vital. It can be 'chunked' as a single unit for connection with our working memory, freeing up valuable capacity for focus on other strands of the Reading Rope.

Teaching a broad, cumulative curriculum will help to build pupils' background knowledge and vocabulary. You can use what you know about progressive sequencing and schema theory (the idea of conceptual webs in long-term memory, discussed in the cognitive science section) to help pupils build cohesive banks of background knowledge. They can then draw upon these quickly when reading a range of texts.

This helps pupils not only to contextualise narratives but also to comprehend non-fiction texts more easily.

Using the Reading Rope to develop inference skills

When analysing reading assessments, we often see questions categorised as testing literal retrieval skills, vocabulary, inference, prediction or summary. Many teachers will want to include all of these discrete question types in reading comprehension tests at the end of Key Stage 2, so pupils have plenty of practice at answering them. However, it is important to remember that inference questions essentially ask the reader to work out 'missing' information in the text, based on clues the author has given us and also information the author assumes we know. As Willingham (2017) explains, our ability to make inferences from a text is strongly dependent on our background knowledge of the content. This is because we rely so much on 'situation models' to fill in the missing pieces.

Situation models

We create situation models as we read a text (Willingham, 2017). They help us to make sense of the words and phrases, and to understand how sentences are connected to give us the 'main idea' of each paragraph. A situation model is a type of schema.

Situation models are temporary connections we make when trying to make sense of a situation. As we read a text, we draw on our schema to build a fuller understanding of the words on the page and their deeper meaning.

For example, if the opening sentence of a story includes the words 'the sun rose over the snow', a reader's schema may tell them it is likely to be a cold winter morning. If a relevant schema (such as understanding of weather patterns) didn't exist, it would be much harder to build a situation model and pick up clues about the setting. Equally, if a pupil didn't have a mental model related to a particular text type, for example a science report, it would be important for you to explain the structure to them before they read the text.

It's important for you, as English lead, to understand this, because it will influence your curriculum design and how sequences of reading lessons are structured. So, what elements of situation models are the most important for us to consider for teaching English?

Situation models help readers go deeper

We use schema to build situation models that help us understand a text beyond surface level. The more background knowledge we have about how texts are structured, and other techniques authors use, the easier it becomes to create situation models for the text we are reading.

Suppose we know that stories typically introduce key characters in the beginning chapters, and that these characters often face and overcome a series of challenges. Knowing this helps us to predict that, when Charles Dickens takes time to introduce and describe Oliver Twist as a sickly infant, for example, Oliver is likely to defy the odds and overcome some big challenges. We know this because it follows a typical pattern: Dickens would not bother introducing Oliver early on if he were not going to be a key character.

Similarly, we can use our knowledge of hooks in story structures to look out for authorial techniques that build foreshadowing, giving us clues to later events. This in turn helps us to understand why closure is so important in narratives.

For non-fiction texts, if we know that scientists analyse data against existing research, for example, we will be able to make inferences about how a report will be structured. Teaching pupils subject-specific vocabulary for a report's particular topic, and providing simple scientific reports related to that area of study, will build their background knowledge in a way that helps them to create situation models quickly. This will in turn help them make sense of the text and comprehend it beyond a surface level.

As English subject leader, you will want to consider how to introduce different plot types and authorial techniques to pupils across year groups. This will require sequencing in long-term planning, and also making sure *teachers* have the background knowledge of the plot types and authorial techniques that are specified.

Building situation models through wide background knowledge

Stanovich & Cunningham (1993) measured the reading abilities of 268 pupils on standardised reading tests, and compared their performance against a range of cultural literacy tests. The cultural literacy tests asked questions about artists, entertainers, military leaders, musicians, philosophers, scientists and various other people from cross-curricular fields. They also included questions on factual knowledge of science, history and literature. The researchers found robust correlations between the scores from the reading and cultural literacy tests: pupils who scored highly on one also scored highly on the other.

Ensuring we teach a broad and balanced curriculum that builds children's cultural capital helps them to become literate of the culture in which they live. This helps ensure they have relevant background knowledge to read and comprehend a wide range of texts. We can build children's cultural literacy by reading a lot – not just novels in English lessons but including non-fiction texts that build children's background knowledge to support their understanding of the context of the novel. We can also read non-fiction texts in other curriculum subjects.

Rather than designing individual reading lessons that focus on inference questions, the evidence base strongly suggests that our pupils are better served by reading texts that build their vocabulary and background knowledge and help them create situation models to 'fill in the gaps' or make inferences.

In summary, as English lead, it is worth considering how much pupils are reading in English lessons and across the curriculum. We can think of this as building 'reading miles'. Shifting our emphasis to reading lots of fiction and non-fiction texts and away from reading short extracts and answering multiple comprehension questions will be a far more rewarding experience for pupils; it will support their reading comprehension much more than practising answering multiple inference questions every reading lesson.

Tips for subject leaders: building cultural literacy to support situation models

You could draw on the following ideas when increasing the breadth of texts in your reading curriculum.

- Consider the types of texts read in each year group, and ensure there is a good cross-section of text types. Be sure to include fiction, poetry and non-fiction. (Chapter 4 discusses how a reading canon can support this.)
- Balance novels with complete short stories, which help to build pupils' knowledge of plot types, story arcs and specific authorial techniques. If pupils experience only extracts, we are not teaching them how to read and analyse a text fully to comprehend it. However, if pupils only ever read short stories, they miss out on so much literature and the joys of an unfolding plot.
- Focus on how you will build pupils' vocabulary and background knowledge. Most new vocabulary is learned through reading: the more you read, the more you learn.
- Challenge pupils to record their 'reading miles' for every subject, not just English. Cross-curricular focus will develop their vocabulary and background knowledge.

Literacy knowledge

Literacy knowledge is a strand within the language-comprehension element of the Reading Rope model: its focus is exploration of books' authors, purposes, intended audiences, genres, publishing contexts and cultural significance. It encourages pupils to 'read around' a text.

Before beginning a new class novel, it can be hugely rewarding for pupils to learn a little about the author: their background, motivations for writing and other texts they have written. A great way to built a text- and talk-rich classroom is to ring-fence time to read the blurbs of other titles by the same author and have copies available for pupils to borrow. It's also important for pupils to learn about the genres to which they are drawn.

Equally, encouraging pupils to share their opinions on texts – including those they are reading beyond the classroom – can be very powerful. All opinions should be validated, but can also be challenged: even if the pupil hasn't particularly enjoyed reading a text, it is positive for them to be able to reflect that they can find good points in it. It helps build their agency.

Recommending further reading

We can further build pupils' literacy knowledge by recommending texts for them to read independently. However, it can be hard for teachers to know which texts to recommend. Research by the Oxford University Press and the UK Literacy Association indicates that many teachers rely on a narrow repertoire of authors. This isn't just new teachers: a highly experienced Year 6 teacher may have a wide repertoire of texts to recommend to their pupils in Year 6, for example, but could struggle with recommendations for a Year 1 class if they moved year group.

It's easy to say that teachers just need to read more children's literature in order to be able to recommend texts to their classes. However, as English lead, you need to be mindful of the demands on teacher time.

One solution to the problem is to introduce class libraries with only about 30–40 books available to borrow at any one time. These books could be taken from your school stock and then rotated throughout the year. Including multiple copies of texts is ideal, as it reduces the number of books with which the teacher must be familiar. It also means that multiple pupils can read the text at once, and they will undoubtedly want to talk to each other about it.

The class teacher could read each text in advance of the start of the term, and introduce them to the class in a reading lesson. Taking time to read the blurb, share a little background knowledge and the merits of each text demonstrates they are valued. In our experience, taking the time to build this kind of culture is more effective and impactful than chasing reading diaries. It also gives teachers time to build their own repertoires of texts worth recommending.

Another way to build teacher knowledge of texts is to set up reading groups at school: the Teachers' Reading Group project set up by the Open University and UKLA (see the 'Explore further' section at the end of this chapter) suggests productive starting points.

Building vocabulary

In Chapter 6, on early reading, we looked at how to select vocabulary worth teaching explicitly, recommendations for teaching vocabulary and example lessons. Vocabulary teaching remains at least as important at Key Stage 2: in fact, Tim Rasinski suggests that 80% of comprehension relies on it.

At Key Stage 2, vocabulary instruction can still draw on the principles below. Teachers should:

- use their professional judgment as to whether they will explicitly pre-teach specific, high-leverage words before encountering them in the text, or read the text first and then explicitly teach the vocabulary
- prepare child-friendly definitions
- use examples of the word linked to the context of the word in the text and then to pupils' background knowledge.

Implicit vocabulary instruction

As we discussed in Chapter 6, it's not possible to teach all the new words pupils will come across explicitly. At Key Stage 2, implicit vocabulary instruction is particularly important. Using implicit instruction, the teacher simply gives a brief definition of the word – or just a familiar synonym or antonym – and the reading continues.

Relying on dictionary definitions can lead to misconceptions: the definitions are often vague because they're context-free. In our experience, definitions from EAL dictionaries tend to be more useful, because they provide contextualised examples.

It's worth noting that the National Curriculum for England and end-of-KS2 TAFs require pupils to use dictionaries to check definitions and spellings, so we need to ensure some curriculum time is spent teaching this. However, as English lead, you should have oversight of how much time is spent looking up words. This time would more productively be spent using teacher-prepared definitions and practising words in a range of contexts.

Using the Reading Rope model to plan a sequence of reading lessons

The Rope Model is not intended to be used as a tick list (for example, to teach background knowledge on Monday, vocabulary on Tuesday and so on). Your aim is rather to build a reading culture in which pupils read a lot and enjoy discussing their responses to the text. It's important to plan reading lessons as a sequence, and be guided by the texts regarding when to draw on a particular Rope strand.

Across our 45 schools, we stipulate core texts that classes have to read from start to finish. The teacher plans in advance the key themes they will pull out as the story of a core text unfolds. This requires that they read the core text a couple of times in advance. Although this may seem demanding, we have found that teachers prefer this approach to reading short, disconnected texts each day. The core texts tend to remain the same so, if a teacher continues teaching the same year group, this approach reduces workload.

In practice: a reading-lesson sequence for *Stig of the Dump*

Because the text to be chosen will guide teachers' choices, it's not possible to provide a template step-by-step sequence appropriate for all texts. Lesson times and allocations also vary from school to school, so the recommendations below aren't framed as discrete lessons.

With those provisos in mind, a sequence of reading phases for studying Clive King's *Stig of the Dump* might look like the example below.

Before starting

- The teacher sources and/or collates a short biographical text about Clive King.
- She prepares child-friendly definitions of the Tier 2 vocabulary that appears in it. (These are high-frequency descriptive and literary words, as discussed in Chapter 6's section 'The importance of building vocabulary'.)

Phase 1: Introduction to the author

- The teacher introduces the author with the short biography, reading it all the way through to model expert, fluent reading. All pupils follow as

secondary readers. This first read gives pupils the gist of what the biography is about.
- To perform the second read, the teacher rereads some sections and calls on different pupils to read others, while everyone else follows the reading in their heads.

Phase 2: Vocabulary instruction and fluency practice

- During the second read, the teacher pauses the reading to explain the Tier 2 vocabulary briefly, using her pre-prepared definitions. She models how to annotate the text with these simple definitions.
- The text is used for fluency practice.

Phase 3: Literacy knowledge

- Basing their ideas on the biography, the class discusses the author's motivations for writing, his historical and geographical context, and the type(s) of text he typically writes.
- The teacher reads *Stig of the Dump*'s blurb, and the class discusses predictions and inferences they can make about the story. They suggest other similar books they've encountered.

Phase 4: Introduction to the core text

- The teacher reads Chapter 1 of the core text as a continuous read, calling on pupils to read parts.
- She takes the class back and analyses some of the figurative language used to foreshadow the fact that Barney will fall into the chalk pit.

Discussion prompts for Phase 4 could include the examples below.

- From our knowledge of typical story structures, what do we know about characters that are introduced early on? (They are main characters.) What kind of thing might happen to them? (They will face challenges.)
- In Chapter 1, we are told that Barney has been warned continually to stay away from the edge of the chalk pit, to avoid falling in. From our knowledge of story structures, what do you think Barney will do?

- Can you identify figurative language that the author uses in the introductory chapter to prepare us for the first challenge the protagonist will face?
- What hooks does the author use to keep us turning the pages during the build-up?

Phase 5: A close read

The teacher spends a lesson close-reading key sections of Chapter 1 to explore the figurative language chosen to foreshadow the events. For example:

> When Barney falls into the chalk pit, we get a sense of death and decay, and King leaves us with a hook to keep reading. Once Barney meets Stig, we realise the chalk pit isn't the dangerous place we initially thought it was. This is a good example of how an author uses hooks to keep us turning the page.

> ### Tips for teachers: don't overanalyse!
>
> You could encourage teachers to draw on the following ideas for performing close reads.
>
> - Overanalysing a text can diminish the joy pupils experience from being immersed in the story.
> - Think carefully about when to take pause points to dig deeper.
> - Once pupils have built schema of typical plot structures and plot points, they will naturally start to look for the clues as they are reading.

Phase 6: Independent reads

The teacher allows time for independent reading of the next chapter(s) of the text. Independent reading should be interspersed with teacher and whole-class read alouds and text discussion.

Tips for teachers: planning independent reads

You could encourage teachers to draw on the following ideas for directing independent reading sessions.

- Plan in regular opportunities for short and longer bursts of independent reading, so pupils can practise reading at their own pace.
- Have a key focus for the reading, and something for pupils to annotate while reading. For example, later in *Stig of the Dump*, you could ask, 'How do we know Barney was excited to return to the chalk pit?' In this instance, pupils should identify that Barney ate his breakfast quickly so he could leave the house.

The balance of reading and text discussion

Talking through how we might structure a series of reading lessons has demonstrated how the text leads the outline of the sequence. By ensuring most lessons are spent reading and rereading texts, we are building reading miles. This, in turn, builds knowledge – particularly vocabulary knowledge. The more background knowledge pupils have, the easier they will find it to comprehend what they read.

Tips for subject leaders: planning reading lessons

You could draw on the following ideas when planning a sequence of reading lessons in English.

- It can be tempting to give teachers a structure to follow for their reading lessons, to make sure they give pupils lots of practice in reading strategies. However, this can easily lead to more time spent answering questions and discussing a text than actually reading it.
- It's important to have a balance of teacher read-alouds, whole-class read-alouds, vocabulary instruction, text analysis and independent reading.
- Most of the time should be spent with all eyes on the text, reading. This may be a shift in approach for some teachers, so it's important

> to consider how to build subject knowledge around evidence-informed approaches to teaching reading.
> - Teachers need to read each text a couple of times in advance, and identify the key points on which they will spend time. These are typically key plot points and themes, literary devices, vocabulary and sentence structures appropriate for the year group.
> - Consider creating a book club the term before a text is read, prompting teachers to read the core texts and pull out these points.

Reading for pleasure: motivation and competency

Reading for pleasure has long been synonymous with building a lifelong love of reading, as well as increased educational attainment (Clark & Rumbold, 2006; Clark & De Zoysa, 2011; Cunningham & Stanovich, 1988). There is much research into the levers that help develop a love of reading, and this identifies motivation as a key factor.

When we experience success, we are far more likely to feel motivated to continue doing something. It therefore makes sense that a reading culture focused on success should help foster reading for pleasure.

Many adults gain much pleasure from immersing themselves in novels. However, we all know adults who are perfectly competent readers but do not choose to spend their leisure time reading. This is the same with children.

Wigfield and Eccles's work on value and self-efficacy support what we have found in practice (Wigfield & Eccles, 2002). Children need to understand and value what they are reading, and to feel successful when reading. Some see the value of reading in order to gain information they need. For others, the value will be immersion in a different world. Unique factors motivate children to read, but reading competency is the key ingredient.

Reading fluency

The role of reading fluency for Key Stage 2 readers

Reading fluency is often seen as the bridge between decoding and reading comprehension. As we explored in Chapter 6, fluent reading requires accuracy, automaticity and prosody. The research strongly suggests that this can be developed through repeated oral practice, which consists of a teacher modelling those skills while reading an extract aloud. Pupils then practise rereading the extract – often to a peer – to build fluency. The extract must be long enough that the pupils are reading and not purely reciting the text (Wolf, 2018).

Text choices for fluency practice

Some researchers suggest that fluency practice is best done with texts that are written for performance, such as poetry, songs and speeches (Raskinski et al., 2016). These formats, however, are less likely than prose to contain the grammatical structures with which pupils need to be familiar. Fluency practice is not just about the words on a page, but also about the punctuation and syntax that make meaning in what is being read (Seidenberg, 2020). Experienced classroom teachers will be aware of pupils whose reading is dysfluent because they do not pay attention to the punctuation that would help them to recognise clause and phrase boundaries. It is therefore important for us to use a range of texts for reading-fluency practice.

Addressing reading difficulties

Good decoding but poor reading fluency

You may encounter pupils who are able to decode words but cannot read as fluently as their peers. This is called hyperlexia. In this instance, extra fluency practice is needed.

However, before taking pupils out of class for fluency practice interventions, it is important for you to consider the amount of fluency practice that takes place in daily reading lessons. It is also important to understand that any additional fluency practice should be short and regular: 5–10 minutes every day for 4–6 weeks will be far more impactful than 30 minutes a week for a year.

In practice: fluency interventions

A quick fluency intervention session could look like the example below.
- The teacher identifies a group of pupils demonstrating traits of hyperlexia, and makes a note of them ready for a same-day intervention.
- She schedules time for the intervention at the end of the day, organising for a teaching assistant to supervise pupils getting their coats and bags.

- During the intervention, the teacher gives the pupils a short, challenging text that takes one or two minutes to read fluently, and models reading it expertly.
- She directs the pupils to practise rereading the text, checking that they progress to become increasingly fluent.
- The teacher makes a note to call on these pupils regularly in the following reading lessons, to ensure they get regular practice.

For more information on hyperlexia, see 'Explore further' section at the end of this chapter.

Good reading fluency but poor comprehension

In contrast, you may encounter pupils whose decoding and fluency skills are in line with those of their peers, but who still have reading difficulties. For these pupils, discrete instruction in comprehension strategies may be beneficial.

The strategies commonly assessed in English were touched upon earlier in this chapter, in the section on developing background knowledge for inference. They are usually considered to be literal retrieval, vocabulary, inference, prediction and summary. As we have seen, these skills are not most effective when taught discretely; rather, they are usually integrated into lessons that are driven by a text. They are also always interlinked: summary is impossible without literal retrieval, for example, and prediction relies on inference.

Nevertheless, interventions that target each strategy individually can help to reveal which pose most problems for pupils. While reading a range of texts, pupils should be taught and encouraged to use and recognise the strategies. Understanding each will help both you and them to monitor their comprehension: you and they will understand what they do not understand. If possible, you can then use the links between strategies to improve skills: for example, if a pupil struggles with summary, you could model combining information collected by literal retrieval. As an initial step, teaching pupils how to summarise a text will ensure they are paying deep attention to what they are reading.

If pupils are not using reading strategies already, they will benefit hugely from this intervention. It is, however, time-limited. Once the strategies have been explicitly taught, pupils need to build reading comprehension through reading miles: reading a lot in all subject areas (Willingham, 2017, p. 126).

Just as for pupils with poor reading fluency, you as English leader need to consider how teachers identify pupils who are reading behind their peers. You also need to ensure that class timetables are organised to allow keep-up and catch-up interventions to take place daily.

Case study: creating a positive reading culture

Hassan is an English lead in a large multi-form-entry junior school in Suffolk. To improve English provision in his school, he decides to hold 'pupil voice' sessions with members of each year group.

Hassan identifies that pupils do not talk enthusiastically about the texts they are reading. Younger pupils do not remember the authors they have read. Older pupils are not able to express any preferences or make connections between texts they have read. When speaking to teachers, he also finds that they do not fully understand the importance of daily story time to model fluent expert reading.

Hassan understands the value of a reading canon, and the importance of cultivating a reading culture in which pupils discuss their reading and make recommendations to each other. He speaks to his line manager about next steps. They agree he should investigate how reading lessons are structured and how daily story time is ring-fenced across the school. He completes his investigation as follows.

- Hassan holds an audit of class timetables to see when reading lessons are scheduled. He looks at planning to see how sequences of lessons are structured.
- He ensures that senior leaders drop into classes at those times during their daily walkabouts. They feed back that:
  - not all teachers are reading aloud to model fluent expert reading
  - story time often falls off the timetable at the end of the day
  - not enough time is spent with eyes on text, reading
  - there are very limited opportunities for pupils to discuss books they are reading beyond the classroom.

  In response, Hassan implements several changes. He:
- runs a short PD session for all teachers to explain two priorities: modelling expert fluent reading and timetabling one session a week for teachers and pupils to recommend books to each other

- runs practice sessions with teachers to build their confidence reading aloud
- agrees with the senior leadership team that they will drop into reading lessons to demonstrate the importance and value of the sessions
- decides to build a school reading canon into his action plan. He knows this is a longer-term piece of work, but it means he commits to starting the groundwork this school year.

Chapter summary

- The strands of Scarborough's Reading Rope can inform important practices in Key Stage 2.
- Background knowledge is vital for putting new vocabulary into context, 'filling in the gaps' when making inferences and forming situation webs: schemas that are particularly relevant for a text.
- Literacy knowledge is vital for contextualising a text further. This includes discussing the text's author, purpose, genre and cultural significance.
- Love of reading can be furthered by recommendations for further reading. Class libraries with a limited number of books can help teachers to make informed recommendations.
- Implicit and explicit vocabulary teaching is still vital beyond early reading.
- The greatest factor informing the structure and content of reading lessons should be the text being read.
- Generally, reading lessons should include:
  - literacy knowledge, including discussion of the author
  - teacher and whole-class read alouds
  - discussion of the text's features as well as content
  - fluency practice
  - a close read, exploring figurative language and its effects
  - independent reads.

- Decoding, fluency and comprehension skills are all needed for motivation in reading.
- Same-day interventions should help to address problems in any of those areas. A positive reading culture can be created by prioritising story times and opportunities for pupils to discuss their reading.

Questions for reflection

- Have I experienced a lack of background knowledge, in pupils or teachers, impeding reading comprehension? How does my understanding of situation models explain what was happening?
- What do we currently do to support pupils with comprehension and inference making? How does our school curriculum build pupils' background knowledge?
- Do teachers intentionally model fluent reading? How do I encourage fluency practice in our classrooms? What kind of texts do I select and on what basis?
- How much time in the average school day do we schedule for reading in the classroom? What could I do to further maximise our pupils' opportunity to build reading miles, and to be exposed to high-quality texts across the curriculum?
- How has this chapter supported my understanding of reading as a process, and of the component knowledge that pupils need?
- What do I think the strengths of our current practice are, and where would I like to develop more expertise and competence? How might this impact our future teaching and leadership of English?

Example PD session: building knowledge with the Reading Rope

You could conduct a PD session on building knowledge with the Reading Rope as follows:

TIMING SUGGESTION	SESSION GUIDANCE
Before the session	Ask teachers to bring their planning for one week of reading lessons.
10 mins	Use the table exploring Scarborough's Reading Rope to explain the many strands that make up word recognition and language comprehension.
15 mins	<ul><li>Look at the table together and identify the types of tasks that support each strand of language comprehension.</li><li>Focus on background knowledge. Looking at the planning examples, identify how teachers can build background knowledge.</li><li>Ask: 'How do we build background knowledge in reading lessons in our school?' 'Do we need to make any changes?'</li></ul>
10 mins	<ul><li>Ask teachers to look at their plans, and to identify where they could build background knowledge around the texts being read.</li><li>Ask them to consider and discuss in groups what this will look like. For example, could they give discrete vocabulary instruction, read a short non-fiction extract and/or use images to deepen understanding of abstract concepts?</li></ul>

Explore further

- *Reading Reconsidered* (2016) by Doug Lemov, Colleen Driggs and Erica Woolway
- *Motivated Teaching* (2020) by Peps Mccrea
- The Open University's *OU/UKLA Teachers' Reading Groups*: teacherhttps://ourfp.org/schools-teachers/teachers-reading-groups/
- The Open University's Reading for Pleasure resources: https://ourfp.org/
- *Closing the Reading Gap* (2020) by Alex Quigley
- The Reading Ape's blog: https://www.thereadingape.com/

- The Reading Ape's *Hyperlexia: a deficit or a super-ability?*: https://www.thereadingape.com/single-post/hyperlexia-a-deficit-or-a-super-ability
- *The Art and Science of Teaching Primary Reading* (2021) by Christopher Such (see pp.95–100)
- *Primary Reading Simplified* (2025) by Christopher Such
- *The Reading Mind: A Cognitive Approach to Understanding How the Mind Reads* (2017) by Daniel T. Willingham
- *Reader, Come Home: The Reading Brain in a Digital World* (2018) by Maryanne Wolf

8 Writing

Writing is an incredibly complex process. Pupils need an idea to communicate, alongside a mental model of how this might look as a written outcome. They need to be competent at producing legible handwriting, accurate encoding, grammar and punctuation, textual cohesion, and vocabulary choice. In addition, we want pupils to demonstrate control of language, manipulation of syntax, selection of vocabulary and deployment of language devices, to create the desired effects on the reader. As a result, many pupils find writing difficult (Graham & Perin, 2007; Schumaker & Deschler, 2009). This difficulty extends into teaching.

We touched on the interrelatedness of reading and writing in Chapter 6, when discussing how our writing system developed. We have also, in Chapter 2, discussed how important it is to reduce children's cognitive load. To teach writing in a way that considers this, and is inclusive of pupils at all attainment levels, there is a lot to consider.

This chapter will cover:

- the complexity of writing and what we can do to help
- how curriculums can be built to develop pupils as writers, considering their:
  - spelling and handwriting
  - grammar, sentences and punctuation
  - exposure to content and text type
- research about practical approaches to grammar teaching
- how writing can be taught, including how units and lessons can be planned
- the importance of suitable model texts
- how this might look at school level.

Writing is hard

There is a gap between the development of pupils' capacity to understand texts and their ability to write texts of similar complexity (Byrnes & Wasick, 2009). Nevertheless, the standards of the texts being read is often the one pupils hold in their heads. Consider this alongside the many components of writing, and then add in the creative mind of a young child excitedly wanting to express their ideas. It is easy to see how quickly working memory can become overloaded.

This overload is the factor most likely to be responsible for writing issues that frustrate many teachers: poor presentation, failure to use capital letters and full stops accurately, or switching from a third to first person narrative mid-paragraph. There is just too much for pupils to hold in their working memory for them to be successful in all areas!

Over time, this can have a concerning impact. Because writing is hard, pupils need to be motivated to invest in this challenging activity – yet success is key to motivation (Bandura, 1997). A lack of success despite their hard work – the feeling that their writing is not considered 'good enough' – can seriously impact pupil's self-esteem and so their motivation to keep trying. As teachers and subject leads, we often see this in schools: some pupils, by Year 6, have already disengaged from the learning process. They have identified themselves as 'not good at English', or 'no good at writing'.

What can we do about this?

We can develop pupils' self-confidence as writers by enabling them to experience successes, and to notice them. One of the most important ways we can achieve this is to ensure writing is taught in a manner that recognises and supports pupils' limited working memory. Too often, when it comes to writing, we treat pupils like mini experts. We expect them to produce and then edit polished and embellished writing within a specific genre. This approach, however, is not supported by what we know about children's development: in fact, it may be a barrier to developing their writing competence (Dennis, 2020). Instead, we can anticipate that our novice writers' working memories will become overwhelmed, and we can plan to overcome this.

We can further empower pupils by encouraging them to invest in the act of writing as a continuing creative process. It has the benefit of being completely editable and can be progressively developed. Writing does not have to be perfect first time! When pupils realise that everything they write can be improved through revision, editing and deletion, they can begin to take risks and experiment.

Developing great writers

Mastering the components of writing will ease the load on pupils' working memory, but will take focused practice over time. Some components are strongly rule-driven, such as the formation of letters (handwriting), spelling, grammar and punctuation. Pupils will benefit from practising these until they are automatised. This means your curriculum should identify what pupils should practise, and ensure teachers have plenty of classroom time for them to do this.

Other components of writing, such as language selection and syntax, offer a significant variety of options. These are the elements about which we *do* want pupils to think hard, in order for them to develop their own authorial voices. Pupils who are able to draw on strong schemas will be better equipped to transform their plans into text and to write with confidence in a range of contexts. A curriculum that supports this will include plentiful opportunities for exposure to, and discussion of, varied models and scaffolds.

Developing a curriculum for writing

Curriculum directives for writing should reduce unwanted cognitive load and thereby support our pupils to become better writers. We have identified four important principles that can be applied, as detailed in the table below.

PRINCIPLE	COMMENTARY
1. The taught curriculum should provide clear, well-planned opportunities for pupils to learn and practise the components of writing.	These components can usefully be grouped into: • handwriting (see Chapter 9) • spelling (see Chapter 10) • grammar and punctuation. We shall explore the categories of components in more detail in this and subsequent chapters.

PRINCIPLE	COMMENTARY
2. The curriculum should limit the number of new components being introduced at a time, and ensure that pupils are not expected to do things they haven't yet been taught.	This limitation applies only to what we ask pupils to do explicitly. EYFS pupils should have opportunities to manage their own mark-making and writing within continuous provision. In other year groups, some pupils may write with a competence beyond that of your intended outcomes. These pupils can still do so and be congratulated for their efforts. The difference is that we should not expect pupils to do things we haven't taught them yet, nor should we assess them as lacking for being unable to do those things.
3. Curriculum sequencing and progression should ensure that pupils have a good knowledge of the content about which they are asked to write.	Later in this chapter, we explore how we can reduce pupils' cognitive load by drawing on prior learning to select content and stimulus for their writing.
4. The curriculum should specify that pupils are explicitly taught that writing is a dynamic process.	Pupils should be taught how to structure, plan, draft, revise, edit and share their work in a non-linear manner.

The spelling curriculum

Just as learning to decode is essential to reading, learning to encode (or spell) is essential to transcription. Pupils won't be able to engage with the creative process of writing if they have to break off every few minutes to check spellings. For this reason, it is useful to develop a spelling curriculum that specifies what spellings will be taught and assessed as pupils progress through your school.

Just as pupils' overall capacity for writing lags behind their reading competence, their encoding levels are unlikely to match their decoding levels (DfE, 2013). Appendix 1 of the DfE National Curriculum for England (2013) provides a helpful starting point in mapping out a spelling curriculum. You should, however, consider this content alongside the sequence of your phonics scheme to ensure you are building on previously taught code. The National Curriculum shifts the focus from the alphabetic code to word lists from Year 3 onwards, but there is no reason why teaching cannot continue to emphasise and develop code knowledge as you teach spellings.

Chapter 10 offers detailed guidance on evidence-informed approaches to the teaching of spelling. It also includes tips for analysing pupils' work to refine curriculum plans and teach responsively.

Why should your curriculum include grammar?

The term 'grammar' refers to the structural rules governing the composition of clauses, phrases and sentences. Within any language, there are certain conventions; typically, individuals internalise the grammar of their native language through exposure (Chomsky, 1965).

This knowledge is, therefore, tacit to the majority of us. We know how to sequence words into an order that enables us to be understood, even if we can't explain the rules or use grammatical terminology. You can consider this by thinking about the grammatical conventions governing the order we use attributive adjectives. If somebody invited you to 'look at those old beautiful five vases' you would sense it sounded wrong even if you didn't explicitly know the conventional order for adjectives. (This is quantity, quality and then age: 'look at those five beautiful old vases' sounds far more natural.)

Could we, therefore, argue that schools do not need to teach grammar at all? Can't we just rely on pupils' tacit knowledge?

Our experience leads us to advise against that position, for reasons that include the following.

- All schools support diverse cohorts of pupils, and some (including pupils with SEND and EAL requirements) will lack the level of English grammar knowledge we may assume is tacit. It is our job to address these gaps, ensuring all pupils have the same chance of success at school.
- Writing is typically more formal and structured than spoken language, demanding greater levels of clarity and precision than are usually needed in speech. Some pupils may internalise the grammar conventions of writing through exposure to texts, but we cannot assume this.

- Explicit grammar teaching can support better written communication. Managing the complex rules governing writing enables pupils to express themselves in increasingly accurate and sophisticated manners.

The Key Stage 2 Standard Assessment Tests (SATs) currently feature an assessment of pupils' spelling, grammar and punctuation. Even in a school that does not follow the National Curriculum, it is highly likely that grammar is taught in some form. It is useful, therefore, to consider how we can best use grammar teaching to support pupils' writing.

What does research suggest?

Grammar-focused programmes

Researchers analysing grammar-focused teaching programmes theorise that these are most effective when learning is both discussed and applied.

Debra Myhill's crucial research established the importance of integrating grammar instruction within the context of writing, and of exploring its effects (Jones et al., 2012). Myhill's view is that grammar teaching can support metacognition by helping pupils use and discuss their grammatical choices. In agreement, the EEF promotes the use of metacognition as an effective way to support pupil progress, particularly the progress of pupils from lower socio-economic backgrounds (EEF, 2021).

Expressive Writing is also a scripted Direct Instruction (DI) programme created by Siegfried Engelmann. The programme, developed as an intervention for struggling writers, uses principles that are effective for all writers by focusing on grammar as a tool for improving writing composition. Every lesson in the programme contains oral and written practice with immediate teacher feedback to secure accurate knowledge. Pupils write sentences and develop short paragraphs, which they then have the opportunity to check and edit.

The standards for DI programme publication are high, as the programmes are extensively field tested. They do not reach market until the lowest performing participants are able to achieve 90% or above on the skills taught within the programme.

Sentence-level writing

There is robust evidence that combining sentences is effective in developing pupils' writing (Andrews et al., 2004; Graham & Perin, 2007). This is an approach advocated by Bruce Saddler, Special Education specialist and author of two books on writing. It involves offering pupils plenty of structured practice forming and manipulating sentences so that writing becomes more fluent, easing the load on working memory. Pupils are gradually supported to secure their understanding of what a sentence is, and to develop awareness of the impacts of their choices (Sadler, 2012).

In practice: what does sentence-combining look like?

A teaching session on combining sentences may look like the example below. Managed well, this approach can shift pupils away from a focus on the surface-level features of sentence variation. It can move them instead towards the use of varied sentence types closely tied to effect.

- The teacher presents pupils with two or more spoken or written kernel sentences (sentences that each express a simple thought). For example:
  - The cat was hungry.
  - The cat greeted its owner.
  - The cat was affectionate.
- The teacher then invites pupils to combine the sentences in a variety of ways. They could form, for example:
  - The cat was hungry and greeted its owner affectionately.
  - The cat greeted its owner, being affectionate even though it was hungry.
- Pupils are given time to compare and discuss their choices, exploring the varying effect of different combinations.
- When pupils succeed, the teacher guides them onto more-complex constructions.

The Writing Revolution, or 'Hochman Method' (Hochman et al., 2017), also features a close focus on explicit sentence-structuring instruction that's supported by plenty of deliberate practice. Pupils are encouraged to correct fragments and run on sentences, unscramble sentences and expand kernel sentences using additional detail. Sentence combining and the 'Hochman Method' can be embedded across the curriculum, particularly as a tools for children to summarise their learning.

In practice: making sentence corrections

Exercises that practise sentence corrections may look like the examples below. These can be integrated into all lessons, as methods for checking understanding or retrieving prior learning. This would ensure there are lots of opportunities to write during the school day.

Correct the fragment

The teacher presents pupils with an incomplete sentence, and asks them to complete it with a subject or verb. For example:

… because it was hungry.

Unscramble the sentence

The teacher presents pupils with a scrambled sentence and asks them to rewrite it. They could start pupils off by suggesting they identify a suitable subject and then hunt for the verb. For example:

was greeted hungry by the and affectionately cat its owner.

Expand the kernel

The teacher presents pupils with a kernel sentence and asks them to complete it. For example:

The cat was hungry so …

Grammar, sentence-writing and punctuation in a programme of study

In our schools, a master document identifies the key learning indicators (KLIs) for writing across each year group. These are mapped out within three categories:

- structure and grammar
- punctuation
- sentence types:
  - statements, questions, commands and exclamations
  - simple, compound and complex sentences.

We have drawn on the National Curriculum for England Programmes of Study to identify these, but have also mapped out the components within the broader writing curriculum. This has made it easier to link the expectations explicitly to the actual writing we expect pupils to produce. Our plans also enable us to highlight knowledge that must be secure by the end of each year. This clarity helps us enable pupils to access the following year's curriculum, providing a clear and helpful focus for teachers.

We also provide subject-knowledge guides for teachers, to ensure shared understanding of terminology. This helps to ensure teaching points and language are used consistently, avoiding confusion for pupils.

The following example table shows Year 3 sentence-level key learning objectives.

SENTENCE LEVEL		
STRUCTURE AND GRAMMAR	TYPES OF SENTENCE	PUNCTUATION
Pupils should be able to: • identify main clauses • identify subordinate clauses • identify phrases • differentiate between phrases and clauses • identify complex sentences • identify sentences that open with words other than nouns or pronouns (e.g. adverbs or prepositions) • write sentences that open with adverbials • write sentences that open with prepositions indicating when or where an event occurred.	Pupils should be able to: • identify and use questions accurately • identify and use rhetorical questions accurately • identify and use commands accurately • identify and use exclamations accurately • write complex sentences using conjunctions: when, before, if, after, while, so, and because.	Pupils should be able to: • identify and explain apostrophes for contraction and possession (singular and plural) • use apostrophes for contraction • identify inverted commas used for speech • use inverted commas accurately for speech.

SENTENCE LEVEL		
STRUCTURE AND GRAMMAR	TYPES OF SENTENCE	PUNCTUATION
• maintain a consistent tense across writing: simple present, simple past, present progressive, present continuous or present perfect • group ideas into paragraphs.		• identify and use commas after fronted adverbials.

The following table shows a Year 3 teacher guide extract.

TYPE OF SENTENCE	DESCRIPTION
Simple sentence	• A simple sentence is formed of one main clause. • It expresses only one action or state of being.
Compound sentence	• A compound sentence is formed of two main clauses joined with a coordinating conjunction. • The most-common coordinating conjunctions in English are 'for', 'and', 'nor', 'but', 'or', 'yet' and 'so' (FANBOYS).
Complex sentence	• A complex sentence is formed of a main clause and one or more subordinate clauses. • A subordinate clause relies on a main clause to make sense. • A subordinate clause, with its conjunction, can go before or after a main clause, or be embedded within it. • The most-common subordinating conjunctions in English are 'after', 'although', 'as', 'because', 'before', 'even though', 'if', 'since', 'though', 'unless', 'until', 'when', 'whenever', 'whereas', 'wherever' and 'while'.

Content for writing

A further way we can free up pupils' working memory is to ask them to write only about things they already know well. We visit schools regularly and often see writing lessons in which very little writing appears to be taught, or to be happening. Instead, pupils are researching new topics or being given extracts from unfamiliar texts to use as writing models.

This can be very challenging for both teachers and pupils to manage. Teachers often find the time they can dedicate to actual writing is reduced. Pupils often find that the challenge of getting to grips with new content can overload their working memory and distract them from the craft of writing.

Rather than take this approach, we recommend the following approaches:

- Draw on the wealth of knowledge taught in foundation subjects to provide interesting content for writing lessons. For example, previous topics on habitats in science, or suffragettes in history, could provide excellent content for simple reports or essays.
- Use a current or recent class reading text as a model for narrative writing. For example, pupils could explore descriptions of fantastic characters or settings as springboards into a piece of descriptive writing.

Text types

Particularly if you are following the guidance of your national curriculum, you will need to ensure pupils have the opportunity to produce writing for a range of audiences and purposes. We recommend that you identify these explicitly within your curriculum map. This will help you to ensure text types are introduced and revisited, and also give you the opportunity to build up a bank of models and resources to support teaching.

Developing a writing curriculum

Long-term plans

Once you have considered the content knowledge you want to cover with pupils, you can start to consolidate ideas into a long-term plan. Our experience is that bringing teachers together to undertake this is a useful way to draw on their expertise of teaching their year groups. It also gives a sense of ownership over the plans and alleviates individuals' workload.

In practice: a long-term plan for writing

A planning map for writing could look like the example below.

YEAR	WRITING OBJECTIVES	EXAMPLE WRITING TASKS
EYFS	• Teachers focus on word-level and then sentence-level writing. • Phonic knowledge and letter-formation skills are developed.	• Write sentences that are dictated (see the chapters on spelling and handwriting).

KS1 (Y1)	• Pupils have further practice writing at sentence level.
	• Pupils produce and manipulate multiple sentences featuring taught grammatical features.
	• Pupils sequence sentences into short paragraphs.
	• Pupils produce simple narratives or reports.
		• Write a simple first-person narrative based on *Goldilocks and the Three Bears*.
		• Practise:
		  • writing with capital letters to begin sentences
		  • writing with full stops to end sentences
		  • writing with past-tense action verbs.
		• Write a simple report that explains what the gunpowder plot was.
		• Practise:
		  • writing using state-of-being verbs
		  • writing consistently in the past tense.

KS2 (Y5)	• Pupils have continued practice combining, editing and manipulating increasingly complex sentences.
	• Pupils produce plans to scaffold longer pieces of extended writing.
		• Write a description of a setting based on *Beowulf*.
		• Practise:
		  • writing expanded noun phrases that include prepositional phrases
		  • using appositives
		  • writing sentences with varied structures
		  • writing using personification
		  • using different paragraph lengths to create mood.

YEAR	WRITING OBJECTIVES	EXAMPLE WRITING TASKS

	• Pupils can produce longer narratives and expository texts, and begin to write analytical essays.	• Write an explanation of what happened when you added each solid to the liquid.
		• Practise:
		  • using a whole-text planning template
		  • planning using individual paragraph outlines.
		• Write an essay exploring how Will changes between the beginning and end of *Goodnight Mr Tom*.
		• Practise:
		  • writing appositives within parentheses
		  • using conjunctive adverbs to link paragraphs
		  • writing introductory and concluding paragraphs.

Teaching sequences

Once a long-term plan for writing is established, teachers can use it to plan their units and lessons. This is not a linear process: skilled writing involves moving between the stages at sentence, paragraph and whole-text levels.

In practice: a teaching sequence for writing

A Year 4 teaching sequence for writing could look like the example below. This structure incorporates the evidence presented above and supports pupils to work through the process of planning, drafting, revising, editing and publishing work.

STEP	PLANNING/TEACHING TASK	EXAMPLE
1	Identify teaching focuses for the unit. These will be drawn from your school programme of study or your national curriculum.	• Write compound sentences using semi-colons. • Write complex sentences that open with a main clause followed by a subordinate clause.
2	Using the long-term plan, identify the text type and knowledge stimulus you will use, and the audience, purpose and narrative perspective on which you will focus.	Text type: Narrative writing Stimulus: *The Firework-Maker's Daughter* Audience: Children 6–12 years old Purpose: To entertain Perspective: Third person
3	Write or identify the extract you will use as a model, ensuring it includes examples of your focuses. Prepare to deconstruct and discuss your model with the class. If you write it, be sure to relate it to the knowledge stimulus you're using.	'The display continued to amaze the crowd although they had already seen more than they expected. It was amazing; cheers and cries rang out.'
4	Identify any prior learning that is a necessity for success in the lesson.	• Independent clauses • Main clauses • Subordinating conjunctions
5	At the start of each lesson, set a quiz or similar quick activity to check prior learning is secure. If you find it is not, prepare to reteach it. Referring to planning earlier in the curriculum should help.	Short quiz testing pupils' ability to: • circle conjunctions • underline main clauses once • underline subordinate clauses twice • add a conjunction and subordinate clause to a main clause.

6	Share the model text with the class. Explore its structure, intended audience and purpose. Discuss how these factors have affected the writer's choices.	Purpose: To convey a powerful description of the fireworks display
		Structure:
		Full text of 5 paragraphs:
		  1. Opening
		  2. Build up
		  3. Dilemma
		  4. Resolution
		  5. End
		Each section of the model only contains previously taught grammar or that within the teaching focus.

STEP	PLANNING/TEACHING TASK	EXAMPLE	
7	Discuss the full text type's structure with the class.	Text template:	
		Opening	•
		Build up	• •
		Dilemma	• •
		Resolution	• •
		End	•
8	Explain what grammar and punctuation you will teach. Allow pupils opportunities to explore the effects of these features by combining sentences, manipulating syntax and building their own bank of diverse examples. Include lots of oral rehearsal, experimentation and discussion of effect.	Teach: Provide and deconstruct lots of representations (models) of complex sentences with the class.	
		Scaffold: Provide specific conjunctions you want pupils to use, including the one(s) in your model ('although'). Ask pupils to practise using them until they achieve a high success rate.	
		Construct: Ask pupils to apply their learning in order to expand kernel sentences.	
9	You are now moving into the text construction stage. With reference to Step 6, guide pupils to build their plans for new texts with the same structure as the knowledge stimulus. Show pupils how turn their plans into complete texts, one step at a time.		
10	• Together in class, construct a new model for each step of the text. Model an ongoing editing process as you write and ensure you include at least two examples of your teaching focuses. • Direct pupils to explore constructing their own steps, drawing on their own banks of examples.		
11	Guide pupils to use their plans and drafts to produce their texts. They need time to draft and redraft: in doing so, they are practising and consolidating their knowledge. At this stage, they are internalising the process you have modelled and monitoring their writing. This increases the chance they will be able to apply what they have learned later across the curriculum. You can provide scaffolding and support, including guided writing, for pupils who would benefit at this stage.		

Models and modelling

Providing models and modelling are essential components of every writing lesson. Teachers use them to deconstruct texts, present contextualised knowledge to pupils and to pull them apart to help pupils build a toolkit for writing.

The models themselves may be single sentences, multiple sentences to be combined into paragraphs, or complete texts. If teachers work through multiple examples with their pupils over a series of lessons, the pupils will then have a bank of models on which they can draw when constructing their final drafts. This offers scaffolding and security to pupils who need it, but also challenges higher-attaining pupils. These pupils can then be asked to use grammatical constructions or key vocabulary in a variety of creative ways.

Preparing model texts

Due to the lag between reading and writing competences, we need to take care we don't expect pupils to produce texts that are as complex as those they are capable of reading. Teachers may seek to use extracts from pre-published texts as their models, and some appropriate passages may be found. However, if teachers have undertaken the writing themselves with close attention to the target knowledge, the models will be precisely tailored to their pupils' learning needs.

To avoid overloading pupils' working memory, you can encourage teachers to write models that:

- include only vocabulary, grammar and punctuation that has either been previously taught (and is secure) or is the teaching focus of the unit
- avoid new, unfamiliar content knowledge that could prove distracting; models should draw on previously taught content knowledge instead.

This may sound simple but is, in our experience, surprisingly difficult to do – which really highlights the cognitive demands that writing places on our pupils. It has significant benefits for teaching, though, as we can pre-empt the difficulties pupils are likely to experience. As subject leader, you will need to consider the workload implications.

> ### Tips for subject leaders: creating model texts
>
> You could draw on the following ideas to help teachers manage the workload of preparing model texts.
>
> - Teachers could work together to produce model texts for the half term ahead. This could be incorporated into your school's professional development schedule.
> - If you are fortunate enough to be part of a network of schools, such as a multi-academy trust or federation, you could team up across the network to share out the work.
> - Save model texts for future use. This means a growing bank will become available, and teachers will be able to draw from it over time.
> - Consider whether any of teachers' other tasks could be put on hold so they can write models instead. This may include detailed marking of books: they could instead look at books to help them identify learning points to include in the models. Alternatively, you could delay administrative work (such as cutting out worksheets or updating classroom displays) that might not be as useful.

- Make sure to communicate to your teaching team that this approach front-loads the work. Teachers will no longer need to search for or create model texts for individual lessons, so they will likely notice they are eventually saving time.

How might a curriculum for writing be implemented?

Pulling together all of this information to create a practical and effective whole-school plan for writing is not as daunting as it sounds. Beginning with evidence and planning backwards can create an effective approach within a clearly structured and directive curriculum.

Case study: an evidence-informed writing curriculum

Stanley Road Primary is a two-form-entry school in Oldham, Greater Manchester. The school's proportions of pupils from lower socio-economic backgrounds and/or with SEND requirements are both higher than average. Around 85% of pupils' first language is not English.

Deputy Headteacher Andrew Percival and Lead Practitioner Jess Rennie have developed an evidence-informed school writing curriculum. Their work provides an excellent model of leadership in English. The table below outlines their approach and why it is likely to be effective.

WHAT HAPPENS?	WHY IS THIS EFFECIVE?
Andrew and Jess have developed a 'Sentence Knowledge Curriculum' based on freely available resources from completemaths.com. This features a granular sequence for the grammar teaching they believe is necessary to develop pupils' writing. Approximately 20 elements of grammar knowledge have been specified for each year group. Pupils are given plenty of explicit teaching and opportunities to practise so they can master each step.	• The curriculum has set out the component knowledge necessary for writing. • The sequenced approach enables teachers to build on pupils' prior learning with explicit teaching. • The mastery approach should enable pupils to develop automaticity. This will free up cognitive load when they later apply the knowledge in their own writing.
This grammar-focused curriculum sits alongside the school's writing curriculum, setting out what texts pupils will write and a clear focus for each. Pupils are asked to write only about topics of which they already have secure knowledge: either texts they have already read or knowledge acquired in other subjects. For example, pupils in Year 4 may write essays exploring ancient Egyptian religion (studied in history) or Varjak Paw (their reading text).	• Pupils' cognitive load is reduced because they are asked to write only about secure subject matter. • Time is used efficiently in writing lessons: it is spent on writing rather than on researching unfamiliar topics, reading unfamiliar texts or self-generating content.

For the first two weeks of each writing unit, daily writing teaching focuses on new knowledge from the Sentence Knowledge Curriculum. Following introduction, teachers provide and discuss model sentences with pupils. They model thinking out loud about the new content, and present a number of examples.	• Narrated modelling develops metacognition and understanding of grammatical choices' impact. • Focused practice establishes high levels of accuracy before pupils move on. Although not a guarantee of long-term retention, this is more likely to be effective than moving on before competence is achieved.
Pupils rehearse sentences orally before writing. Activities include a range of sentence-expansion and -combining activities, with an aim for 100% accuracy in writing before moving on. Teachers are encouraged to spend more time on this stage when necessary.	• Oral rehearsal can help pupils organise their expression, whilst enabling self-reflection and peer feedback. • The high level of accuracy expected means all pupils keep pace with the learning.
The teacher models collating sentences to create longer pieces of writing. Their models feature the target grammar, alongside that previously taught and literary devices for effect and vocabulary. Teachers cycle between modelling and practice multiple times, gradually removing scaffolding as pupils become more confident. Pupils continue to rehearse sentences orally before writing.	• Further modelling continues to develop metacognition and understanding of grammatical choices' impact. • Consolidation of new content sits alongside retrieval of prior learning. • Highly scaffolded working progresses to more-independent writing with support.
In the final weeks, pupils write independently. They discuss, plan, draft, edit and finalise their work. They then read it aloud to a partner to check it.	• Pupils continue to narrate their thinking. • They benefit from self-reflection and peer feedback.

Andrew and Jess ensure teachers are provided with detailed guides to enacting the curriculum. These sequentially set out: • all the knowledge required • the model texts and example sentences to use • each unit's entire teaching sequence for Weeks 1–6 • sentence-knowledge teaching tools, with examples drawn from the curriculum. They provide further support by organising professional development time for developing the grammatical and linguistic knowledge teachers need, and for staff to co-plan model texts.	The guidance builds teacher expertise, establishes consistency around language, lesson expectations and content, and provides a blueprint for professional development that focuses on clear curricular and teaching techniques.

Chapter summary

- Writing is a creative act and success plays a powerful role in building self-confidence and motivation.
- The limits on pupils' working memory need careful consideration. Mental models and automaticity with component knowledge help pupils to transcribe their ideas.
- We can develop pupils' expertise as writers by carefully sequencing the components of writing, teaching these explicitly and giving pupils plenty of opportunities to practise.
- Embedding grammar teaching into a whole-school approach to teaching writing may support pupils' metacognition, enabling them to monitor the quality of their own work.

- Cognitive science research suggests that sentence-level mastery can improve pupils' writing and ease the load on working memory.
- We can reduce unwanted demands on working memory, improve quality of writing and increase pupils' engagement by asking pupils to write about content they already know well. We can draw on reading texts and knowledge from the wider curriculum.
- It is vital to ensure that all teachers understand your plan for progression and how to enact it.
- Models play an integral part in the development of pupils' writing competence. They should focus closely on target knowledge, limiting exposure to knowledge not already taught.
- Effective writing curriculums should be clearly structured, specific about what knowledge to teach when, and informed by evidence.

Questions for reflection

- How much time do teachers have to secure sentence-level writing practice in the curriculum? Do reviews of pupils' work suggest they have enough practice at this level to master the basics of writing sentences? If not, how might I need to review the curriculum to allow for this time?
- Do our teachers already teach how to combine sentences? If not, what support, training and development might they need to develop this?
- Does our writing curriculum set out, in enough coherent detail, not just what pupils will write, but also what writing component knowledge they need to be taught? Does it indicate clearly what areas of prior learning might be appropriate as writing stimuli?
- How can I plan to support teachers to write good model texts, accounting for the workload this involves?

Example PD session: co-creating a writing curriculum

You could conduct a PD session on co-creating a writing curriculum as follows:

TIMING SUGGESTION	SESSION GUIDANCE
Before the session	Teachers will need a good understanding of the curriculum for their year group, and a solid sense of how this fits into the whole-school curriculum for writing. You will need: • your writing curriculum: the grammar, punctuation, language feature and sentence knowledge you will teach in each year • your reading curriculum: the texts pupils will read in each year • your wider curriculum: the topics covered in foundation subjects in each year • sticky notes • copies of 'A long-term plan for writing' in the 'Content for writing' section of this chapter • large copies of an unpopulated table in the format of the 'long-term plan for writing' (as below).

YEAR	WRITING OBJECTIVES	EXAMPLE WRITING TASKS
EYFS	e.g. Focus on word-level and then sentence-level writing.	e.g. Write sentences that are dictated.
Y1		
Y2		
Y3		
Y4		

		Y5		
		Y6		
10 mins	Explain that you will be working together to: • identify what you will ask pupils to write in each unit across a year • identify the knowledge that will need to be taught within each unit • identify the secure content knowledge on which pupils will draw for their writing • co-create a long-term plan for writing.			
40 mins	• Ask teachers to sit in year or phase groupings, and to begin identifying suitable writing tasks and stimulus content for their year groups. • Prompt teachers to organise the component knowledge under the headings on the table. This will take some trial and error, and even debate: sticky notes may help to enable this exploration and flexibility.			
20 mins	Place the plans for the different year groups side by side from EYFS to Year 6. Ask teachers to sense-check the whole sequence by considering: • Have we included plenty of opportunities for oral storytelling in EYFS? • Would this sequence give pupils the opportunity to write for a good range of audiences and purposes? • Is the content knowledge we propose to teach well sequenced? • Will pupils have enough opportunity to practise and revisit this knowledge? • If pupils learn this content successfully, will they become better writers? • Have we missed anything?			
After the session	Use the planning to produce your overarching writing curriculum.			

Explore further

- The points on developing pupils' writing in the EEF's *Improving Literacy in Key Stage 2* (2021)
- *The Writing Revolution* (2017) by Judith C. Hochman & Natalie Wexler, with Kathleen Maloney
- The Writing Revolution's site: https://www.thewritingrevolution.org/
- *The Teacher's Guide to Effective Sentence Writing* (2012) by Bruce Saddler
- Stanley Road Primary School's 'Sentence Knowledge Curriculum' and 'Writing Curriculum': https://www.stanleyroad.oldham.sch.uk/english.html
- Stanley Road Primary School's webinar on their approach and the impact: contact the school via their website: https://www.stanleyroad.oldham.sch.uk/english.html

9 Handwriting

In this chapter, we will unpick the skill of handwriting. This transcription skill is often described as 'secretarial', because it is seen as less-challenging than composition. Composition – choosing what and how to write – is more cognitively challenging. However, every teacher encounters pupils who struggle with handwriting. This is because, when we are learning the skills of handwriting, they take up a lot of our working memory: they are hugely cognitively challenging.

You can get a good sense of this if you try writing your name in an unfamiliar script. For example, if you're used to writing in English (with the Roman alphabet) and you try writing your name in Greek (with a Cyrillic script) or Panjabi (with the Gurmukhi script), you will find your handwriting is laboured. This is because you will need to refer to a script chart to remind you of the shape of each symbol. Without instruction, you won't even know where to begin it. You will be unable to repeat spelling your name correctly without lots of practice.

Equally, if you do not have a comfortable tripod grip and relaxed wrist when writing, you will tire quickly when you are practising your letter formation. Handwriting instruction needs to be planned strategically, and with a deep understanding of its precursors, to ensure this does not hinder pupils' writing.

In this chapter, we will cover:

- why handwriting instruction matters
- the developmental stages of handwriting
- developing the skills necessary at each stage
- layering handwriting practice over secure phonic knowledge
- ways to assess possible handwriting schemes.

Handwriting instruction: why it matters

Handwriting and reading success

For handwriting to become fluent, we need to be able to form letter shapes without consciously thinking about them. Research evidence indicates there is a strong link between handwriting fluency and reading: pupils who write letters fluently in Year 1 are likely to be better readers than those who do not (Ray et al., 2021; Young et al., 2015).

Handwriting and writing success

Handwriting fluency is more obviously linked to writing success (Santangelo & Graham, 2016). Pupils without fluent handwriting can become easily frustrated when they are not able to write down everything they want to express. When handwriting is fluent and unconscious, pupils can focus more freely on the cognitively more challenging compositional aspects of writing.

The EEF's 2021 guidance report on improving literacy in Key Stage 1 emphasises the importance of regular and substantial practice with effective feedback, including the correct starting point for each letter. The Ofsted English education subject report found that, despite this, most schools do not give pupils enough teaching and practice to develop high degrees of handwriting fluency, and that dictation is rarely used as tool to practise handwriting and spelling (Ofsted, 2024).

Teaching handwriting

The sequence below shows a path through stages to fluent handwriting. Knowing the developmental sequence will help you not only to guide pupils' progress, but also to identify what the best intervention may be, if necessary.

It is important to note that, in all cases, teaching handwriting discretely in regular short sessions is likely to be more successful than using longer, less-frequent lessons. Aiming for five to ten minutes of instruction followed by five to ten minutes of practice at least three times a week is ideal. These sessions should, also ideally, be held outside of phonics lessons as well as within them.

Pre-writing skills

Before developing fluent handwriting, pupils need to develop their pre-writing skills. These progress from simple hand and finger movements to forming lines, circles, squares, crosses and triangles. From there, once pupils are able to hold and move pencils fluently, they can learn to form letter shapes and produce legible writing.

Pupils who have not learned pre-writing shapes by the time they begin phonics lessons can be given magnetic letters to spell words in phonics lessons. However, their pre-writing skills should continue to be developed.

The table below presents examples of activities that develop pre-writing building blocks. The building blocks are not sequential, and many activities will develop more than one.

BUILDING BLOCKS	ACTIVITIES TO SUPPORT DEVELOPMENT
Hand and finger strength	Scrunching paper, using pegs and manipulating salt dough
Crossing the midline	Dance routines, ball sports, balance boards and gymnastics
Pencil grasp	Using tweezers and placing pegs in peg boards
Hand–eye coordination	Throwing and catching balls, hitting balls with a bat, and threading
Bilateral integration	Scrunching paper, using scissors and exploring musical instruments
Upper-body strength	Climbing ladders and wheelbarrow walking (for upper-limb strength)
Object manipulation	Drawing, painting, doing puzzles, threading and opening containers
Visual perception	Drawing dot-to-dot pictures, identifying objects in feely bags and matching pairs
Hand dominance	Observation and reinforcing of dominant-hand strategies (with parental support)

BUILDING BLOCKS	ACTIVITIES TO SUPPORT DEVELOPMENT
Hand division	Playing with tiny objects such as buttons and small shells (to develop ability to use 'spare' fingers for stabilising)

It will be important to provide activities like these beyond EYFS for pupils who have difficulties with writing readiness: some of those pupils may also need opportunities to develop gross motor skills and core strength. As well as building pre-writing skills, the activities will allow you to observe pupils to identify where the difficulties lie. For pupils in older year groups, you can adjust the tasks to make them more age-appropriate.

Teaching print

As pupils acquire pre-writing skills, they can be taught to form individual letters correctly in a printed script. The DfE guidance document *Validation of systematic synthetic phonics programmes* (DfE, 2023) states that, when first learning to write, pupils should not be taught to join letters or to start every letter with a lead-in. They also recommend that all resources designed for pupils to read should be in print. Alphabet posters with printed script capital and lower-case letters, without lead-ins, are helpful for reinforcing the letter formations pupils are learning.

An effective way to teach letter formation is to introduce the letters in phonics lessons first. This means that pupils can see that the letters represent sounds in words, and that their focus is on reading. Separate, discrete handwriting sessions should then be held later each day, focusing on how to form the letters taught in earlier units. Revisiting this teaching a couple of weeks later allows for spaced practice and, in terms of cognitive science (as discussed in Chapter 2), embeds understanding. Pupils will already know what each letter represents in a given word, so they can focus all their attention on how each letter is formed.

Learning handwriting is most effective when we teach motor patterns (air writing, for example) rather than visual patterns. Teaching a 'patter' for each letter can be a useful tool to support correct letter formation and internalising the motor patterns. This involves a series of (often fun) descriptive instructions for how a letter is formed. For example:

- To form 't': Draw down the tree, curve the roots and then cross the branches.
- To form 'r': Rain down to the ground; curve over the rainbow.

Some handwriting schemes include patter, and we have included a free-to-access example in the 'Explore further' section. It is key to ensure that all teachers and pupils across the school use patter consistently.

It can also be helpful to model letter formation using patter and then using handwriting repeater software to record this. (A free option is suggested in the 'Explore further' section at the end of this chapter.) It works well to set this to replay the formation on a loop, while you circulate to support pupils as they practise writing the letters. As you circulate, you can watch for correct starting points as well as further formation.

It's also important to teach the subskills listed below explicitly, checking for them until they become automatic.

SUBSKILL	HOW TO PRACTISE IT
Directionality	You could support development with activities such as painting with water on the playground, using large chalks, air writing and tracing in sand.
Tripod pencil hold or grip	Once habits form, it is very hard to correct poor pencil grip: be extremely vigilant that this is modelled regularly and practised correctly in KS1. You may like to teach pupils a little script to help them remember how to hold the pencil. This could be as simple as BBC Bitesize's 'point, pencil, pinch', or as elaborate as one of the many 'Crocodile' songs that can be found online.
Posture and paper position	Model placing the paper sloped along the line of the writing arm, off-centre from the midline of the body. Pupils should sit at appropriately sized tables and face the board straight on as much as possible.

Teaching joined handwriting

Once pupils can form printed upper- and lower-case letters automatically, they are ready to learn a joined script. This usually begins in Year 2. For schools with mixed Years 1–2 classes, it is important to be clear with pupils when you are teaching print for Year 1 and when it's a joined script for Year 2. Encouraging pupils to join letters before they have correct, automatic formation of print letters will impede the development of a fluid joined script. Making this progress is important, though: using joined script develops muscle memory that's related to spatial and physical awareness and also supports both reading and writing.

Your handwriting lessons will be strongly influenced by the programme you follow. However, most teach letters in similar orders. These are likely to begin with letters that start like 'c': those that start on the line with a diagonal join. Next will likely be letters that end with a loop join: 'o', 'r', 'v', 'w' and 'x'. Finally, schemes will revisit some instances of letters like 'c', which begin with a loop instead of a diagonal join if they are joining letters that end with loops: 'c', 'a', 'd', 's', 'g', 'o' or 'q'.

Considerations when choosing a handwriting scheme

Although their sequencing may be similar, it is important for you to be aware of handwriting schemes' approaches to this, and to other factors. The table below suggests some you should consider.

FACTOR	CONSIDERATIONS
Sequencing	Does the sequence build systematically? How quickly are pupils introduced to all the letter joins? Is regular practice built in?
Modelling	Does the scheme provide sufficient information and support on how to model individual letters and groups of letters?
Scripted handwriting patter	Is there a simple script for patter to help pupils remember where to begin, continue and end each letter? Does the scheme include plans that show how and when to use it?

Implications for the classroom

The case study below shows how an English lead used this knowledge to improve handwriting in his school.

> ### Case study: improving subject knowledge on handwriting development
>
> Joe is an English subject lead in a three-form-entry primary school in Cardiff. The school's phonics programme has a handwriting element, but this is used only up to Year 1. The school uses pen licences in KS2, to encourage pupils to write neatly. Handwriting is timetabled for 30 minutes weekly.
>
> In a learning walk, Joe identifies that many pupils in all classes have poor handwriting. Further investigation identifies that teachers often use handwriting lessons as holding activities so they can focus on other interventions, such as reading with small groups. Joe knows from his reading that this is not the most effective practice. He believes that building subject knowledge amongst staff will help him to change the school's approach to teaching handwriting.
>
> Joe shares his findings with his school's headteacher. She agrees that he should build staff's subject knowledge, and then research handwriting schemes. Using his knowledge of the evidence base for best practice, Joe creates a document to outline a whole-school approach to teaching handwriting. He schedules a short series of PD sessions for teachers on the developmental stages of handwriting.
>
> During these sessions, Joe shares his document with teachers. He also asks them to identify pupils in their classes with handwriting difficulties, and to consider the interventions most likely to benefit them. Joe supports teachers as they work in phase groups to consider how they can adapt their handwriting lessons.
>
> Over the next weeks, as teachers practise their subject knowledge, Joe researches handwriting schemes.

Chapter summary

- Fluent handwriting is a prerequisite for writing composition. Once this skill is automatic, working memory is freed to work on the complex task of composition.
- For the same reason, fluent handwriting supports better spelling.
- Five minutes of daily practice is more effective than 30 minutes once a week.
- Gross motor skills need to be developed before fine motor skills. A range of activities can develop both of these.
- Understanding the developmental stages of handwriting development will help you to guide pupils' progress. It will also help you to identify the most useful interventions, if needed.
- The sequence of learning to transcribe is from pre-writing, to writing print, to writing joined letters.
- Handwriting schemes should be considered carefully in terms of provision for modelling, sequencing, patter and phonics alignment.
- It is vital that teachers have a good understanding of handwriting's developmental stages.

Questions for reflection

- Do teachers have the opportunity to ensure pupils have sufficient practice to develop fluid, automatic handwriting?
- How will we identify and support pupils who need more practice?
- How will I develop teachers' ability to do this?
- How could I use the development stages of handwriting to identify the starting points for handwriting interventions?

Example PD session: developing handwriting skills

You could conduct a PD session on developing handwriting skills as follows:

TIMING SUGGESTION	SESSION GUIDANCE
10 mins	Use the 'Teaching handwriting' section of this chapter to help explain the developmental stages of learning to write.
15 mins	• Ask teachers to identify pupils in their classes who have poor handwriting. • Ask teachers to consider the 'Teaching handwriting' information to identify where barriers may lie for those pupils. • Discuss the importance of modelling and practising correct pencil grip, and the impact if this is not secured early on. • Discuss the importance of modelling correct letter formation. Are all teachers secure with how to do this? • As a team, answer this question: How will we ensure we practise correct pencil grip and letter formation in every lesson?
10 mins	Ask teachers to work in small groups to model pencil grip and letter formation. They should model writing complete print or joined words (using your school's handwriting patter, if relevant). Ask them to take turns until everyone in the group has taught a mini lesson.

Explore further

- The strands on handwriting in the EEF's *Improving Literacy in Key Stage 1* (2021) and *Improving Literacy in Key Stage 2* (2021) reports
- HFL Education's *How to help with handwriting* (2023) by Juliet McCullion: https://www.hfleducation.org/blog/how-help-handwriting
- CT Games's free handwriting-repeater software: https://ictgames.com/mobilePage/writingRepeater/index.html

- Debbie Hepplewhite's free handwriting programme for examples of handwriting patter: http://debbiehepplewhitehandwriting.com/free-resources/

10 Spelling

In this chapter, we will unpick the complexities of learning to spell. All too often, we see teachers asking pupils to edit their work with partners, and look up incorrect spellings in a dictionary – only to see the words still spelled incorrectly in later learning. This is because they are approaching spelling as the seemingly simple task of error correction. They aren't using what we know about how learning happens, or about connections between code knowledge and spelling patterns.

When spelling familiar words, we usually rely on muscle memory. We have written the word so many times that we have learned the spellings to the point of automaticity, and can write them fluently. When we try to spell an unfamiliar word, we invariably hesitate. We break the word into chunks and use our knowledge of existing spellings in our attempts to spell it.

That is only the best scenario, though. Many of us will have seen pupils instead choose a simpler word to write because they do not know how to spell the more sophisticated alternative. They may write 'cash' rather than 'money', for example, or 'big' instead of 'huge'.

In this chapter, we will cover:

- teaching spelling through secure phonic knowledge: encoding and decoding
- why contextual writing is important for learning spellings
- how pupils' cognitive load can be reduced by a focus on word parts: both syllables and morphemes
- how an understanding of etymology can put spellings into context.

Teaching spelling through secure phonic knowledge

Spelling is a much harder skill to master than reading. Whereas reading requires only recognition memory, spelling requires us to recall from memory actively

(McGuinness, 2006). We have to recall our phonic knowledge and decide which grapheme is the correct one for each phoneme. For example, if spelling 'they', pupils need to remember to use the 'ey' spelling of /eɪ/ rather than the more-common 'ay' spelling.

In Chapter 6, on early reading, we touched on the history of writing. Here again, it's important for us to understand how writing developed. It helps us to fathom the reasons why there are different ways to spell one sound, and so to appreciate the importance of secure phonic knowledge.

Establishing more-common spelling patterns

When pupils move beyond learning the initial one-to-one correspondences in CVC (consonant–vowel–consonant) words such as 'dog' and 'tip', they are introduced to CVCC words such as 'jump' and 'luck'. At this point, teachers can introduce the idea of blending consonants, as with /m/ /p/ in 'jump'. They can also introduce 'digraphs': two or more letters that represent just one phoneme, such as 'ck' in 'luck'.

In tandem, teachers can introduce the idea that some spelling patterns are more common than others, and that some appear in only certain places in words. For example, when teaching 'luck', teachers can explain that words in English never begin with 'ck'. Pupils can be introduced to the fact that some spelling patterns are more common than others, and so they are more likely to be correct.

Structuring practice

It is important to note that, as for all new knowledge (as discussed in earlier chapters), spaced practice is constructive. By practising the spellings of words a few weeks after pupils have learned the phonic code to read them, we embed the sound–spelling correspondences for reading as well as writing. Phonics programmes that incorporate spellings should sequence this for you, but it is worth checking and considering adjustments if this is not the case.

> **In practice: spaced practice for phonics units**

A structure for spaced practice of phonics units could look like the example below.

PHONICS LEARNING PHASE	WEEKS 1–2	WEEKS 3–4	WEEKS 5–6
Oral introduction to new code, with pupils using white boards or magnetic letters	Unit A	Unit B	Unit C
Practice of the taught code through reading texts	–	Unit A	Unit B
Application of the taught code through spelling dictation	–	–	Unit A

When pupils are in the 'apply' phase, writing short sentences to practise sound–spelling correspondences, it is worth considering the activity as handwriting practice, too.

Ways to teach spelling

Avoiding exposure to misspellings

McGuinness (2006) suggests that pupils should not be exposed to examples of lists including misspellings (distractors) and asked to choose correct spellings: this may accustom pupils to the incorrect patterns. Rather, spelling instruction is likely to be most effective when pupils are taught the correct sound–spelling correspondence through direct instruction, and then given lots of deliberate practice through writing the words.

Writing contextually

Several research studies indicate that physically writing words helps us to remember them (McGuinness, 2006). However, learning lists of words in isolation for weekly spelling tests does not automatically translate into accurate spelling in writing. It may be more effective to practise spelling these words within sentence dictation (Gruhn et al., 2019), because our brains favour narrative. Building a schema of a word's meaning and how to use it means we are therefore more likely to use it in context. Ofsted's English education subject report (2024) identified that, despite this, teachers rarely use dictation to help pupils practise their spelling. This was therefore identified as one of their key recommendations.

Avoiding distractions

It can be tempting to try to make spelling lessons 'fun', perhaps by suggesting pupils write with coloured pencils, draw around words or hunt for them in word searches, for example. This, however, increases pupils' cognitive load (as discussed in Chapter 2). Under that strain, the risk is that, rather than learning the letters that spell a particular word, pupils may remember the colours they used or the shapes they drew. The same principle applies to activities such as matching singular and plural words by drawing lines to match them: pupils may remember only the rules of the task.

Working syllabically

As pupils are introduced to polysyllabic words, we can break down spellings by syllable. Focusing on the sound–spelling correspondences one syllable at a time reduces cognitive load. Within one syllable, we can draw pupils' attention to the sound–spelling correspondences with which they are already familiar, and then discretely teach the new correspondences.

When reviewing spelling errors, we can ask pupils which parts of each syllable are tricky for them, and draw their attention to the letters representing the sounds in that part of the word. When you spend time focusing on each part of a word, and allow time for deliberate practice of writing it, you prompt pupils to think hard about a smaller unit of information. This improves the pupil's chances of remembering it and so is time well spent (Willingham, 2017).

As English lead, you should guide teachers to respond to questions about how to spell a word with this syllabic approach. They should ask, 'Which part of the word are you struggling with? What are the ways you know to spell that sound?' If it is a spelling pupils have not yet been taught, the teacher could reassure them, 'We haven't learned that spelling yet. That sound is spelled '…' in this word.'

Teaching spelling through morphology and etymology

Syllabic practice leads nicely to introducing morphology.
The National Curriculum for England states:

Phonic knowledge should continue to underpin spelling after key stage 1; teachers should still draw pupils' attention to GPCs [grapheme-phoneme correspondences] that do and do not fit in with what has been taught so far. Increasingly, however, pupils also need to understand the role of morphology and etymology. (page 39)

Morphology

Morphology is the study of morphemes: a morpheme is the smallest meaningful unit in a word. In the word 'disrespectful', for example, there are three morphemes: 'dis', 'respect' and 'ful':

- The morpheme 'respect' is the root word: it gives the word as a whole its main meaning. Affixes (prefixes and suffixes) can modify its meaning, but they mean nothing without it.
- The morpheme 'dis' is a prefix: it is added to the beginning of a root word to modify the word's meaning. The prefix 'dis', specifically, reverses meaning: in this case, 'disrespect' is the opposite of 'respect'.
- The morpheme 'ful' is a suffix: it is added to the end of a root word to modify the word's meaning. The suffix 'ful', specifically, means 'full of' (often in abstract terms): for example, if someone is 'respectful', they are full of respect.
- Together, someone 'disrespectful' is full of the opposite of respect.

Once pupils know the meanings of morphemes and their purposes, they can build their repertoire of spelling (and vocabulary) considerably. However, it's important that they are taught not to rely on only morphology for meaning. To check meaning, pupils can sometimes simply look for a root word: for example, the word 'disco' begins with letters that form a common prefix, but 'co' is not a meaningful word. At other times, things are harder: 'display' also starts with 'dis', for example, and 'play' is a recognisable word – but 'display' is not the opposite of 'play'.

In practice: teaching morphemes with more than one meaning

A teaching approach to ambiguities in morphology may look like the example below.

- The teacher writes the word 'teacher' on the board.
- She asks two or three pupils, and then the whole class, to read it aloud.
- She points to each syllable in turn, saying, 'The word "teacher" has two syllables: "teach" and "er".'
- The teacher asks pupils to define the word, and clarifies the response simply: 'A teacher is somebody who teaches.'
- She points to the root verb ('teach'), and says, 'Teach: it's what I'm doing now. It's a verb.' She points to the suffix 'er' and says (while stressing 'er' and 'ing'), 'A teach*er* is somebody who does the teach*ing*. "Teacher" is a noun.'
- The teacher continues, 'Today, we're going to focus on how the suffix "er" tells us what a person is doing. Let's say "teacher" in its syllables: "teach-er". Now write "teacher", saying the sounds in each syllable as you do so. Then write and say the whole word.'
- The teacher next writes 'singer'. She again calls on several pupils to read it, before the whole class does.
- She says, 'Based on the fact that a teacher teaches, what is a singer? Tell your partners.'
- After allowing time for discussion, she takes feedback and identifies the suffix for 'singer' is 'er'. She identifies the full noun ('singer') and root verb ('sing').
- She repeats the spelling process: 'Write "singer", saying the sounds in each syllable as you do so. Then write and say the whole word.'
- The teacher writes 'leader', elicits what the verb is and asks pupils to share the definition in pairs.
- After allowing time for discussion, she takes feedback and deepens knowledge as necessary (a 'leader' is someone who goes first or is in charge). She says, 'A teacher is a leader: I am in charge of the class. The first person in a race can be a leader: they are at the front, going first.'
- The teacher asks pupils to use the word in a sentence with their partners (giving them only ten seconds).

- She recaps what 'leader' means, and asks pupils to share the definition with their partners (again giving them only ten seconds).
- She repeats the spelling process again: 'Write "leader", saying the sounds in each syllable as you do so. Then write and say the whole word.'
- The teacher recaps that the suffix 'er' has changed the word each time to mean 'the person who does that thing'.
- She repeats with other words (such as 'player', 'farmer' and 'publisher').
- The teacher writes 'faster' and 'slower' on the board, and elicits that 'er' is now not telling us what someone does. She talks about the root words 'slow' and 'fast' as necessary, reminding pupils that these are adjectives.
- She includes the words in sentences: for example, 'My car is faster/slower than that one.'
- The teacher reminds the pupils that 'faster' and 'slower' are comparative adjectives.
- She recaps that the suffix 'er' can be used both to describe what someone does by changing a root word (verb) into a noun, and to compare something to something else. She drives home that the suffix 'er' can be used in different ways.
- The teacher writes 'steer' on the board, and explains that this word is an 'odd one out'. She asks the pupils to explain to their partners why this is the case.
- After allowing time for discussion, the teacher takes feedback and elicits that 'er' is not a suffix in 'steer'. She draws pupils' attention to this clearly, to avoid them leaving the lesson with any misconceptions.

Etymology

Etymology is the origin or story of a word. As we touched on in the 'How to teach spelling' section above, our brains favour stories. We find it easier to remember a story than isolated facts such as spelling rules or spelling lists. This is because stories make connections to events: the more connections we make with something, the easier it is to remember. (See the discussion of schema theory in Chapter 2.)

To secure some spellings, we can tell their stories. For example, if pupils have problems spelling 'biology' (or any other '-logy') with its 'g' rather than a 'j' or 'dge', you could explain that the ending is developed from a word for writing – like in a 'log book'. Explaining that the Ancient Greek spelling of 'air' was 'aer' can help older pupils to spell words they could identify as relatively technical, especially in science: 'aeroplane', 'aerial', 'aerosol' and 'aerodynamic'.

This approach can also help with more-common affixes. When teaching the prefixes 'a', 'dis' and 'un', looking at the etymology can help pupils understand why one meaning can be created by these different prefixes. They come from different origins: Ancient Greek, Latin and Early Germanic respectively. As older pupils' vocabulary grows, you could use these ideas to make interesting semantic links. The prefixes can usually be paired with words from the same origins:

- The Ancient Greek prefix 'a' forms words like 'atypical'; 'typical' also has Ancient Greek roots. A clue for this origin is in the 'y' for /ɪ/.
- The morphemes 'un' and 'true' both have Early Germanic roots, so stories may be 'untrue'. The spelling 'ue' is a typical for Old Germanic.
- Both 'dis' and 'appear' have Latin origins, so a magician can 'disappear' – which could be a useful phrase in context, as the 'ci' spelling for /ʃ/ is typical of Latin.

Too much etymology can also become confusing, however, so it's important not to make it the 'main thing' in our spelling lessons. Thinking carefully about when it will be most useful, and keeping the primary focus on code knowledge and spelling patterns, will be a key part of our oversight as English lead.

Using etymology to discuss less-common spellings

Considering the complex history of English, we may choose to approach spelling discussions differently. Rather than telling pupils that a word like 'diamond' is tricky or contains a 'silent a', we could explore the word's etymology. 'Diamond' has been used since Middle English and came from Ancient Greek 'adamant' (meaning 'untameable' or 'unbreakable'), via Latin variants 'adamans' and 'diamas', and then Old French 'diamant'.

In practice: putting etymology into practice

A whole-class intervention for correcting a common misspelling could look like the example below.

- An English teacher learns that several pupils in his class have been misspelling 'pyramid' in their history lessons. He decides to spend time in his spelling lesson focusing on the parts of the word pupils are misspelling.
- He writes 'pyramid' on the board, and draws vertical lines to divide the word into syllables: 'py|ra|mid'. He asks a pupil to read the word's syllables distinctly, and then asks the whole class to do this.
- The teacher explains that the term has a long history, and the word as we know it comes from Ancient Greek: 'pūramís' (/puːræmɪs/), which became 'pȳramis' (/paɪræmiːs/) and then 'pȳramidis' (/paɪræmiːdiːs/) in Latin, and then 'pyramide' (pɪʁəmiːd/) in Old French.
- He asks, 'Which parts of the word might be tricky to spell? Let's have a look at the first syllable.' He elicits that 'y' represents the sound /ɪ/ in this word, whereas it more often represents /i/ as in 'happy', 'busy' and 'dolly', at the ends of words.
- He asks the pupils to talk to their partners about any other words they know where 'y' represents the sound /ɪ/. Examples: gym, Olympics, hymn, Egypt. He makes the link that there are pyramids in Egypt. He then explains that all of these words also come from Ancient Greek.
- He looks at the second syllable and notes that the 'a' is pronounced as /ə/ (a schwa). He draws attention to the way 'a' sounds when it's used as an article: 'a pet' or 'a friend'. He points out that we say this as 'ə' too, but we know how it's spelled.
- The teacher rubs out the word and asks pupils to discuss the difficult spellings with their partners.
- After allowing time for discussion, he asks pupils to write the word in their books, sounding it out in syllables first and then saying and writing the whole word.
- The teacher writes the word on the board again, and asks pupils to check their spellings.

Planning for common errors

Your most critical action when working to improve spelling will be to motivate teachers to plan ahead. Integrating spelling interventions into mid-term plans will help them to get ahead of any problems.

Case study: improving the spelling of common errors

Brit is an English subject leader at a small mixed-year-group school in Cambridgeshire. When the school participated in external writing moderation, it was noted that several pupils were spelling high-frequency words incorrectly.

Brit has previously created a spelling Scheme of Work by mapping out the teaching of high-frequency words, spellings in the Appendix of the National Curriculum for England, and spelling patterns by phase (KS1, Lower KS2 and Upper KS2). Brit can see from teachers' planning that they are following the sequence.

When Brit looks at pupils' books, though, she notices that teachers correct only the spellings they have taught. They do not correct spellings taught in earlier phases. Brit shares her findings with her headteacher, and they agree that Brit can lead a whole-staff PD session as follows.

Organisation

Brit prepares copies of:

- Appendix 1 of the National Curriculum for England
- the school's spelling sequence
- their phonics programme progression map
- curriculum maps for the units of study teachers will cover in the next half term, which includes subject-specific vocabulary
- a range of pupil books that demonstrate a range of attainment levels, including books belonging to pupils with EAL and SEND requirements.

PD session

- Brit asks teachers to sit in year/phase groupings.
- She shares copies of Appendix 1 of the National Curriculum for England and the school's spelling sequence. She highlights where commonly misspelled words are taught, and emphasises the importance of responsive teaching if pupils are still spelling those words incorrectly in later years.

- Brit asks teachers to look through pupils' books together, making a note of the common sound–spelling correspondences that they are getting wrong.
- She asks teachers to look for patterns – are there any common errors that could be addressed at whole-class level?
- Teachers continue to work in pairs or groups, and turn their attention to the spelling lists alongside the wider curriculum maps for the next half term. Brit asks them to note:
  - the common or high-utility words on the list that feature the common errors pupils have been making
  - the subject-specific vocabulary words related to the curriculum next half term that feature the common errors pupils have been making.
- Teachers finish the session with time to work independently, to map onto their plans for the next half term and identify which lessons they could use to teach the spellings of potentially problematic words.

Follow-up PD session

- Brit uses the professional development task featured at the end of this chapter to support teachers to plan their teaching of those words.

How many sound–spelling correspondences should we teach?

There are around 200 sound–spelling correspondences in English. To some extent, the story of the English language has illustrated reasons for this.

You do not need to ensure pupils are taught all 200 sound–spelling correspondences discretely. Once they have mastered the majority, pupils will be able to self-teach the remainder through exposure in reading (Ehri, 1995). As pupils' code knowledge secures in Year 2, they will be able to apply their knowledge of affixes, and growing knowledge of morphemes, to 'chunk' parts of words to help in their reading and subsequent spelling (Share, 1995).

It's important to consider how many sound–spelling correspondences should be taught explicitly, though. While you do not need to consider all 200 when planning, teaching only 60–65 can lead to pupils in Key Stage 1 using phonetically plausible – but incorrect – spellings. If not addressed, these habits can become embedded. In our schools, we teach around 150 sound-spelling correspondences in phonics and then spelling lessons.

Most Year 6 teachers will be able to name at least one pupil who continued to spell 'they' as 'thay' because they were not taught the 'ey' spelling for the sound /eɪ/. Decisions around your choice of spelling programme are likely to be closely linked to your choice of phonics programme.

Chapter summary

- Spelling supports reading far more than reading supports spelling.
- Spelling should be structured by a well-sequenced phonics programme that supports spaced practice.
- Learning lists of words has been shown to be less effective than contextual writing.
- Working syllabically can lessen pupils' cognitive load and embed understanding.
- Understanding morphology can help pupils to piece together word parts, including suffixes and prefixes; teachers should, however, consider potential ambiguities.
- An understanding of etymology allows pupils to engage with the stories of words, and can help to explain their tricky parts.
- Planning for common errors can prevent problems persisting at later stages.

Questions for reflection

- How does our phonics programme support our spelling programme?

- How can code knowledge be used to support the teaching of sustained improvement in spelling skills?
- How confident are our teachers with the concepts of morphology?
- Could teaching be developed by a better understanding of etymology? What professional development sessions or resources could support this?

Example PD session: using etymology in spelling lessons

You could conduct a PD session on incorporating etymology as follows:

TIMING SUGGESTION	SESSION GUIDANCE
Before the session	Ask teachers to identify what words they plan to teach pupils to spell during the following week.
10 mins	Use the section of this chapter on the history of English to help you explain some reasons why there are so many different sound–spelling correspondences in English.
15 mins	- Prompt teachers to use a website like 'Etymonline' to look up the etymology of the words they will be teaching. - Discuss how they could incorporate this information into their spelling lessons while following your school's spelling programme. (If you do not follow a spelling programme, you could consider an example outline from the case study in this chapter.) - As a team, answer this question: How will we embed the use of etymology in our spelling lessons?
10 mins	Ask teachers to work in small groups, taking it in turns to teach one word's spelling using their new etymological knowledge. They should rotate the role until everyone in each group has taught a mini lesson.

Explore further

- *The Cambridge Encyclopedia of the English Language* (2018) by David Crystal
- *The Stories of English* (2004) by David Crystal
- The Reading Ape's *English spelling! Do I really have to teach it?*: https://www.thereadingape.com/single-post/english-spelling-do-i-really-have-to-teach-it

11 Purposeful oracy

> Some things impress you the moment you enter a classroom. One of them is being engaged immediately in a confident, nuanced conversation with an erudite pupil: one who knows what they want to say, and how to say it. To some pupils, this seems to come naturally. For most, however, it must be developed using a carefully structured curriculum and expert teaching.
>
> In order to speak confidently, pupils need a deep understanding of the subject about which they are talking. They additionally need knowledge of the vocabulary, language structures and body language appropriate for the type of talk with which they are engaging. This, in essence, is oracy.
>
> In this chapter, we will cover:
>
> - what oracy is
> - how to develop effective oracy, considering different approaches to teaching it
> - components of oracy curriculums
> - the importance of vocabulary for oracy
> - the role of dialogic teaching in English
> - planning for different forms of classroom talk, including paired talk and debating skills.

What is oracy?

Oracy is the ability to talk and listen, and also to learn through and about those skills.

Neil Mercer defines oracy education as direct and explicit teaching of speaking and listening skills within a language and literacy curriculum (Mercer et al., 2019).

The Oracy Education Commission's report on the future of oracy, *We Need to Talk* (2024), identifies the importance oracy in equipping pupils to:

- ask questions
- articulate ideas
- formulate powerful arguments
- deepen their sense of identity and belonging
- listen actively and critically
- understand the fundamental principle of a liberal democracy: being able to disagree agreeably.

Developing effective oracy

Oracy education in the primary years begins with pupils listening to and telling stories, leading to an emerging sense of where they fit into the world. Through a rich primary curriculum, oracy can help pupils to learn more powerfully and deeply as their knowledge is built and expanded by expert teachers.

Within a school's oracy curriculum, pupils will be taught to present as well as discuss their knowledge. This is distinct from oral rehearsal before writing. Written text is often dense and carefully crafted to ensure words and phrases are not repeated. Speech is very different. Talk is transient, and our limited working memory means we need to reiterate key points in discussions. Where we use synonyms in writing, we repeat the same words and phrases in spoken language, to help the listener process our points.

Oracy education should include development of the skills required to participate in paired, small-group and whole-class discussion. It should also include the skills required to declaim speeches, perform poetry, present information and, ultimately, to engage in courteous discussion and debate. We can think of oracy as the skillset for organising that elements of all the types of talk in which we participate. As a result, as English lead, you need to ensure it is clear when pupils are discretely taught these skills.

Approaches to teaching oracy

Learning 'to', 'through' and 'about' talk

Oracy could be approached from many different sets of angles. We have identified three key components: learning how to talk, learning information through the medium of talk and learning about the conventions of different types of talk.

- To develop pupils' learning about how to talk, an oracy curriculum should identify the skills required to be an effective speaker and listener and the specific approaches for different types of talk.
- Oracy as a pedagogy can be seen as the transfer of information through different types of talk. This might be, for example, through conversational philosophical inquiry, comprehension of a presentation or paired talk (Mannion, 2023).
- In order to become a skilled debater or to deliver an effective presentation, pupils need to learn the conventions of each type of talk, as well as having deep knowledge of the subject they are debating or presenting.

The Oracy Skills Framework

Another approach is suggested in Oracy Cambridge's *Oracy Skills Framework and Glossary* (Cambridge, 2019) which identifies a significant body of knowledge underpinning the development of spoken language, for both speaking and listening. It provides a list of key criteria for each of four strands, as below. They suggest that these could be used to frame teaching, and for formative assessment.

Physical:	Linguistic
• Pace of speaking	• Appropriate vocabulary choice
• Tonal variation	• Register
• Clarity of punctuation	• Grammar
• Voice projection	• Rhetorical techniques
• Gesture and posture	
• Facial expression and eye contact	

Cognitive	Social and emotional
• Choice of content to convey meaning and intention • Building on the views of others • Structure and organisation of talk • Seeking information and clarification through questions • Summarising • Maintaining focus on task • Time management • Giving reasons to support views • Critically examining ideas and views expressed	• Guiding or managing the interactions • Turn-taking • Listening actively and responding appropriately • Self-assurance • Liveliness and flair • Taking account of level of understanding of the audience

Four components for a curriculum

An oracy curriculum could also be viewed as a combination of four main components:

COMPONENT	EXPLANATION
Language structures and vocabulary	• These skills are facilitated through a carefully chosen reading canon that contains a wide range of stories, rhymes and songs. • Core vocabulary and sentence structures are identified and taught.
Routines and processes	Routines and processes for structuring talk and listening are taught.
Types of talk	• Pupils are taught how to engage in the conventions of specific types of talk, including explanations, presentations and debates. • As pupils progress, they should learn to speak with more-formalised grammar and register when it is appropriate for different audiences and purposes.
Practice	Pupils practise the skills of oracy regularly, so they can use them competently across curriculum subjects.

The importance of vocabulary in an oracy curriculum

In order to articulate their thinking and reasoning clearly, pupils will need to draw from a vocabulary bank that is both broad (varied) and deep (nuanced and well understood). All too often, we see vocabulary breadth privileged over vocabulary depth, resulting in inappropriate vocabulary choices and misunderstanding of nuances in texts studied.

When you are identifying content pupils will discuss, explain, present and argue, it is important to build in time for discrete instruction on vocabulary for core knowledge. This will include Tier 2 and some Tier 3 vocabulary: high-frequency descriptive and literary words, and low-frequency subject-specific words (as discussed in Chapter 6's section 'The importance of building vocabulary').

In the earliest stages, your curriculum could direct that such vocabulary be introduced simply through pupils' interactions with adults. This may be when discussing texts, by listening to stories, poems, rhymes and songs, and when learning these by heart. In later years, the curriculum should identify when to teach, practise and revisit the vocabulary and ideas needed for effective communication. Opportunities to refine and apply this knowledge in many contexts, including for different audiences, will help pupils to hone their procedural skills. This will, in turn, build their confidence and competence.

Steps for teaching vocabulary in Key Stage 2

The framework for structuring vocabulary attainment below is based on a five-step sequence promoted by Beck, McKeown and Kucan in *Bringing Words to Life* (1987). Although it makes reference to teaching words, it can also be used to introduce phrases.

(In Chapter 6, on early reading, we presented example vocabulary lessons for EYFS and Key Stage 1.)

STEP	STAGE OF VOCBULARY ATTAINMENT
1	Pupils have no knowledge about a target word. For example, in the passage below, they have no knowledge of the word 'mendacious'. 'Her mendacious behaviour made it difficult for me to trust her.'
2	Pupils have a general sense of meaning. For example, they understand that 'mendacious' has a negative connotation.
3	Pupils' knowledge is narrow and bound to context. For example, they have heard a quick definition to aid them in reading the passage of text: 'Mendacious means untrustworthy.'
4	Although pupils remember the word's simple definition, but their knowledge isn't deep enough for them to be able to recall it for use in other appropriate situations. Pupils' examples are likely to be along the lines of these: • 'It's hard to trust a mendacious person.' • 'His mendacious personality was untrustworthy.'
5	Pupils have a rich, decontextualised knowledge of the target word's meaning, its relationship to other words and its extension to metaphorical uses. For example, pupils can compose sentences that reflect the nuances of the word 'mendacious', such as these: • 'A chameleon to the core, the novel's protagonist was known for her wit and mendacious charm.' • 'Always open and honest, Rosa does not have a mendacious bone in her body.'

We have found that pupils' knowledge of many words is limited to Step 4 of the sequence above. By teaching and spending time on Step 5, we move this to a level that will support them to understand complex concepts, and to articulate their thinking with confidence in all kinds of talk situations.

Recent research on the vocabulary found in children's books indicated that 28% of words in books aimed at 7–9-year-olds, and 40% of words in books aimed at 10–12-year-olds, were not present in a sample of CBeebies and CBBC programming that was aimed at children up to age 12 (Korochkina et al., 2024). This further supports the importance of discrete vocabulary teaching that moves pupils' knowledge from Stage 4 to Stage 5: without explicit instruction, pupils may not encounter the words elsewhere.

As we have explored above, the task of reaching Step 5 will be best served by spaced practice: revisiting learning often in the short term, and then exercising recall in the long term. We have found that teaching to a routine – always following the above five steps for understanding, for example, and exercising spaced practice systematically – reduces cognitive load for both pupils and teachers. It gives pupils more time to build a rich schema for each word. This means they will be able to use it readily in their expressive vocabulary, as well as understand the nuances of meaning in their receptive vocabulary.

Components and composites in an oracy curriculum

The Ofsted English subject report (Ofsted, 2024) discusses the concepts of components and composites that we discussed in Chapter 2: granular steps of learning and their more complex end point. We know that pupils are more likely to be successful in their learning if the components are carefully broken down and sequenced, allowing plentiful opportunities for retrieval practice to achieve automaticity.

In practice: granular steps in a oracy curriculum

An oracy curriculum based on granular steps could look like the example below. The steps build from foundational behaviours for speaking and listening in Early Years, and progress to planning, preparing and delivering an argument for discussion in Key Stage 2.

YEARS	KEY LEARNING INDICATOR	GRANULAR STEPS
1–2	The pupil reads out their own sentences as a presentation to a group.	The pupil: • reads out their own work in a clear, confident voice • pauses appropriately at full stops • changes their intonation to indicate feelings • changes their intonation to indicate questions • explains their reasons for these changes in intonation.
	The pupil learns and retells short stories.	The pupil: • retells a story in a clear, confident voice • changes their intonation to indicate a change in mood • changes their intonation to indicate characters • explains their reasons for these changes in intonation.
	The pupil learns and recites short classic poems.	The pupil: • recites a poem in a clear, confident voice • understands the meter of the poem • delivers the poem with the correct rhythm • identifies which words rhyme (if any).
	Core texts to learn and perform: *A Visit from St Nicholas* by Clemente Clark Moore, *The Owl and the Pussycat* by Edward Lear, quotes from *The Tempest* by William Shakespeare, additional poems selected by the school	
	The pupil reads out their completed work as a presentation.	The pupil: • reads out their own work in a clear, confident voice • uses punctuation to indicate feelings • pauses appropriately at commas and full stops • explains their reasons for changes in intonation.

YEARS	KEY LEARNING INDICATOR	GRANULAR STEPS
3–4	The pupil retells a story.	The pupil: • retells a story in a clear, confident voice • changes their intonation to indicate a change in mood • changes their intonation to indicate characters • explains their reasons for these changes in intonation.
	The pupil learns and recites a poem.	The pupil: • recites a poem in a clear, confident voice • understands the meter of the poem • delivers the poem with the correct rhythm • identifies which words rhyme words (if any).
	The pupil plans, prepares and delivers a presentation.	The pupil: • identifies a subject area to present • identifies the audience (including demographic information) • includes an introduction that contains a hook for the reader • includes separate points elaborated with at least once sentence, opening each with an introduction and closing it with a concluding sentence • links points with related connecting phrases (where appropriate) • includes a conclusion that summarises, challenges, emphasises their authority and makes links to the introduction • uses accompanying diagrams/pictures to illustrate points • uses examples to illustrate points • delivers the presentation in a clear, confident voice • pauses appropriately between points.
	Core texts to learn and perform: Jabberwocky by Lewis Carroll, Jim – A Cautionary Tale by Hilaire Belloc, quotes from Richard III by William Shakespeare and, additional poems selected by the school.	

YEARS	KEY LEARNING INDICATOR	GRANULAR STEPS
5–6	The pupil reads out their completed work as a presentation.	The pupil: • reads out their own work in a clear, confident voice • pauses appropriately at full stops • changes their intonation to indicate feelings • changes their intonation to indicate questions • explains their reasons for these changes in intonation.
	The pupil learns and recites a poem.	The pupil: • reads out a poem in a clear, confident voice • changes their intonation to indicate a change in mood • changes their intonation to indicate characters • explains their reasons for these changes in intonation.
	The pupil learns and declaims a Shakespeare soliloquy.	The pupil: • explains that a soliloquy is a speech delivered to oneself • explains that a soliloquy enables the audience to understand a character's thoughts • delivers the soliloquy in a clear, confident voice • understands the meter of the soliloquy • delivers the soliloquy with emphasis on any rhymes (including internal and half rhymes) • identifies which words rhyme (if any).

YEARS	KEY LEARNING INDICATOR	GRANULAR STEPS
	The pupil plans, prepares and delivers a presentation.	The pupil: • identifies a subject area to present • identifies the audience (including demographic information) • includes an introduction that contains a hook for the reader • includes separate points elaborated with at least three sentences, opening each with an introduction and closing it with a concluding sentence • links points with related connecting phrases (where appropriate) • includes a conclusion that summarises, challenges, emphasises their authority and makes links to the introduction • uses accompanying diagrams/pictures to illustrate points • uses examples to illustrate points • delivers the presentation in a clear, confident voice • pauses appropriately between points.
	The pupil plans, prepares and delivers an argument for discussion.	The pupil: • identifies the two sides of an argument • chooses a side to argue • identifies the audience (including demographic information) • includes an introduction that contains a hook for the audience • elaborates the argument's main points, perhaps using a planning frame • includes a conclusion that summarises and emphasises the main argument, perhaps using a planning frame • delivers the presentation in a clear, confident voice • pauses appropriately for effect.
	Core texts to learn and perform: The Listeners by Walter de la Mare, The Schoolboy by William Blake, short scene from Macbeth by William Shakespeare (Act IV Scene I), additional poems selected by the school.	

Reproduced with permission from The Diocese of Ely Multi-Academy Trust and developed from documents created by Angel Oak Academy.

The role of dialogic teaching in English

When thinking about how talk is organised in the classroom, you need to consider the role of dialogic teaching. Dialogic teaching focuses on the quality of classroom talk. Robin Alexander developed the term in the early 2000s, along with a dialogic teaching framework (Alexander, 2018). Alexander identifies that dialogic teaching assumes a conversational manner and involves discussion that is collective, reciprocal, supportive, cumulative and purposeful (Alexander, 2020).

This is all dependent on teachers building a respectful classroom culture in which all pupils feel confident talking. In English lessons, teachers will naturally build pupils' collective understanding of key themes in a text through carefully crafted discussion. By having a clear end point in mind, teachers can give their pupils planned discussion prompts in paired, small-group and whole-class scenarios.

The resulting dialogue can prompt pupils to dig deeper and to explore the nuances of vocabulary and hidden themes in texts. They will be able to reflect more effectively on their own writing and the impact it has. They can also evaluate the ideas of others, providing justifications and elaborations.

Forms of classroom talk

Mercer (1995) studied the types of talk happening in primary classrooms, and grouped them into the four categories detailed below.

- Cumulative talk is characterised by very little challenge. For example, pupils share their thoughts but do not build on what has gone before.
- Disputational talk involves contributions that are competitive rather than collaborative. For example, pupils working on a group project make individual assertions with few attempts to build on each other's knowledge.
- Exploratory talk occurs when groups problem-solve through collaboration and shared purpose. For example, pupils working on a group project use their knowledge of the subject matter to make assertions, critically evaluate them and come to conclusions.

- Presentational talk is employed when the focus shifts from individuals to an audience. For example, pupils use their findings to give a presentation to their peers.

Planning for talk

In primary classrooms, we usually focus on exploratory and presentational talk.

Exploratory talk is most often dialogic: its tone is conversational. However, without careful planning and preparation, exploratory talk – whether between partners, within small groups or involving a whole class – can become unproductive. In our experience, identifying opportunities for this kind of talk at the planning stage helps to ensure it remains focused.

Being clear about the end point for a lesson, and about the prerequisite knowledge necessary for talk to be meaningful, will help to ensure the planned talk is purposeful and aids learning. The example Key Stage 2 reading lesson outlined in Chapter 10 provides an example of the granular steps required when planning for purposeful talk.

Teaching talk routines, with clear expectations of engagement, are best planned in advance. In our trusts, we have thought carefully about the level of detail required, and have codified what we will teach. The example below guides you through some of the considerations for teaching paired talk that our English leads consider with staff.

Teaching paired talk

Paired talk can be especially effective for pupils in EYFS. As well as being a constructive way for pupils to explore their and each other's ideas, it can help to establish the basic skills of oracy: their abilities to express their ideas and listen to those of others.

In practice: teaching paired talk in EYFS

A plan for teaching paired talk might look like the example below.

1. Introduce the content of the talk

- Ensure that pupils already have the knowledge required for them to respond to the talk prompt. This may be relevant background knowledge and/or personal experiences. For example, you could ask pupils to recall the story *Goldilocks and the Three Bears*.
- Supply the talk prompt. This could be a question targeted at personal response, perhaps, or a request for literal retrieval. For example, you could ask pupils to identify three different ways Goldilocks has been or could be described. Alternatively, you could ask a more open-ended question, such as, 'What is your opinion of Goldilocks?'
- You may find it useful to identify key points you expect to hear from pupils, to keep the talk focused and purposeful.

2. Direct pupils before the talk

- Pair up pupils with talk partners.
- You may wish to identify who will talk first. For example, Partner A in each pair may be the pupil who's sitting closest to a classroom feature, such as closest to the window.
- Give pupils clear instructions regarding how long they will talk.
- Establish or remind pupils of your talk routine. This could include:
  - talk positions, such as sitting cross-legged and knee-to-knee, with hands in laps
  - using a 'talking stick' so partners take it in turns to speak
  - having a 'stop' routine, such as counting down from three before pupils should turn to face you, making eye contact to show they are listening.

3. Conducting the talk

- Circulate to observe paired talk, listening in to pick up on key discussion points. This will help you to get a general sense of pupils' thinking, and to select pupils to share discussion points with the class.

- Be aware that talk facilitated by a teacher will naturally last for longer than pupils talking independently. This may lead to some pupils not staying focused as their talk peters out.
- Keep the talk short. Allowing just a minute will enable you to incorporate paired talk more frequently, and mean pupils can share and develop their thinking regularly.

4. Moving on to whole-class dialogue

- Referring again to your talk prompt, ask pupils to feed their ideas back to the class.
- To increase accountability, we find creating a no-hands-up or all-hands-up culture helpful. This means pupils know that anyone could be called on to share their ideas, and keeps everyone on task.

Teaching debating skills

Older pupils' oracy can be exercised and extended by the development of debating skills. Before thinking about the nuanced skills themselves, though, we need to ensure that the prior learning is secure: pre requisite knowledge not only of the topic to be debated, but also of basic oracy practices such as taking turns to talk, building on what a previous speaker has said, tone of voice, body language and eye contact.

Neglecting this can mean lessons with a strong oracy component become less effective for some learners. Those with strong subject knowledge of the project content, and a clear understanding of how to prepare and present a presentation, will be far more successful than pupils who do not have this knowledge. In our experience, this will lead to the Mathew Effect (the rich get richer, and the poor get poorer): the pupils who need the most practice gain very little from the learning.

Case study: developing the teaching of debate

Jaala is an English subject lead at a one-form-entry school in Norfolk. When reviewing how the school teach oracy, she finds that:

- key poems to learn and perform were specified for all year groups
- pupils present short reports across both Lower and Upper KS2
- pupils participate in debates in Upper KS2.

Generally, pupils perform poetry and present reports competently. However, the quality of oral debates, particularly in Year 5, is variable: the pupils prepare their arguments loosely, on topics from only their general knowledge, rather than using scaffolding or focused research.

Jaala shares her concerns with her line manager, and talks to the Year 5 teacher about the scheme of work used. They identify that the teaching steps are not sufficiently granular. They also discover that not all pupils have sufficient vocabulary and background knowledge for the topics debated, so they can't form and articulate their arguments coherently.

Jaala decides to address the problems by spending some of her English release reviewing the granular steps for teaching debate across Years 5 and 6. She and the Year 5 teacher, Jim, work together to plan a sequence of learning that they can trial.

Jaala and Jim prepare the model debate plan below, and record themselves enacting it. They write up their dialogue as a script.

DEBATE QUESTION: In Lewis Carroll's *The Lion the Witch and the Wardrobe*, is Edmund good or bad?		
Debate structure	Additional notes	Worked example
Response	Consider the question and decide your viewpoint.	Edmund is good.
Introduction	Give a simple response to the question as a summary of your viewpoint.	Edmund is immature and easily led, but ultimately good. The witch has manipulated him.

Developed point(s) (NB: For UKS2, one point is sufficient.)	Explain the main reason(s) why you hold your viewpoint, and present evidence in support.	• There is good in everyone. • Edmund is humble when he first meets the witch. • He shows concern about being lured into a trap when he's following the robin. • His actions during the final battle show him taking responsibility.
Examination of the other side	Present opposing evidence and explain why you reject it.	Edmund denied entering the forest. However, he was already under the witch's spell after eating the Turkish delight that she offered him.
Anecdote	Make an appeal to audience, such as a relatable experience that may connect the audience to the issue.	Who can turn down their favourite delicious treat?
Summary	Summarise your key points.	It takes the actions of a good person to overcome the witch's spell. In the end, good won.

Jaala and and Jim plan for Jim to teach the following English lessons.

- Jim shows the recording while identifying the key parts of the structure. He then hands out copies of their script and asks pupils to practise performing it, encouraging them to show some of the granular skills in the oracy curriculum (such as reading in a clear, confident voice).
- Pupils are asked to write balanced arguments based on their class novel, *The Lion, the Witch and the Wardrobe*, to use as starting points for an oral debate.
- Groups supporting the same side of the argument practise presenting their points together, and then the debate is held.

> Jaala plans to review this trial, further developing the scheme of work to include sequences of granular steps. The scheme will also specify that oral debating will be taught in English lessons across Upper Key Stage 2.

Chapter summary

- Oracy is about expressing and listening to ideas, including forming arguments, considering information critically and being able to disagree politely.
- It also includes understanding the context of talking and listening, including the requirements of different forms of expression, purposes and audiences.
- An oracy curriculum should start with granular components and work towards composite learning goals.
- The Oracy Skills Framework is a useful starting point for planning the granular steps that need to be taught within four strands: physical, linguistic, cognitive, and social and emotional oracy.
- An oracy curriculum should progress from basic routines for speaking and listening to more-complex forms of talk, such as debate.
- Dialogic teaching uses dialogue in a conversational manner to develop understanding of a topic.
- Planning ways to use dialogic talk in the classroom ensures that talk remains constructive.

Questions for reflection

- How is oracy taught in our school? What do I think the strengths of our current practice are, and where would I like to develop expertise and competence?
- How confident are we in teaching oracy effectively? Do we feel we have a training or development need in this area?

- When and how is the composite knowledge for oracy taught? Do teachers know which procedural knowledge has been taught previously, and which they should teach their year groups?
- How has this chapter supported my understanding of forming an oracy curriculum? How might this impact on my future teaching?

Example PD session: building progression into the oracy curriculum

You could conduct a PD session on the importance of building progression into your oracy curriculum as follows:

TIMING SUGGESTION	SESSION GUIDANCE
Before the session	• Ask teachers to bring bullet-pointed lists of how they teach performance poetry in their year groups. • Lay out the lists from EYFS through to Year 6.
10 mins	• Show the granular steps and precise sequencing of the example oracy curriculum in the 'Components and composites in an oracy curriculum' section of this chapter. • Explain the importance of building progression into the oracy strand of your English curriculum, and use performance poetry as a starting point.
15 mins	• Ask teachers to look at the points for performance poetry in their plans, and discuss similarities and differences across the school. • Identify the sequence of performance-poetry teaching and discuss how the performance expectations become more demanding over time. • As a team, answer this question: 'How do pupils make progress in performance poetry in our school?'

TIMING SUGGESTION	SESSION GUIDANCE
10 mins	• Ensure teachers understand the importance of spaced practice for oracy, in the context of performance poetry. • Agree on the key steps to take when developing pupils' progress and reiterate to colleagues how this looks for each year group.

Explore further

- *A Dialogic Teaching Companion* (2020) by Robin Alexander
- The EEF's *Preparing for Literacy: Improving Communication, Language and Literacy in the Early Years* (2018): https://d2tic4wvo1iusb.cloudfront.net/production/eef-guidance-reports/literacy-early-years/Preparing_Literacy_Guidance_2018.pdf?v=1737642976
- *Classroom Talk: Evidence-based Teaching for Enquiring Teachers* (2020) by Rupert Knight
- *Oracy: The State of Speaking in Our Schools* (2016) by Will Millard and Loic Menzies https://cfey.org/wp-content/uploads/2016/11/Oracy-Report-Final.pdf
- Oracy Cambridge's *Oracy Skills Framework and Glossary* (2019): https://oracycambridge.org/wp-content/uploads/2020/06/The-Oracy-Skills-Framework-and-Glossary.pdf
- The Oracy Education Commission's *We Need to Talk* (2024): https://oracyeducationcommission.co.uk/wp-content/uploads/2024/10/Future-of-Oracy-v23-web-13.pdf

12 Monitoring and quality assurance

> The term 'quality assurance' (QA) represents the systems and procedures that are intended to maintain a good quality of education across a school.
>
> As English subject lead, your QA processes should enable you to make decent inferences about pupils' education in English at your school. A really good QA system can also do more than this. If the system is well designed, the information you glean from it can help you celebrate achievement as well as identify and work with others to keep making improvements to pupils' education.
>
> In this chapter, we will explore:
>
> - the pitfalls of QA and how to avoid them
> - the importance of building a positive QA culture
> - guidance on QA regarding:
>   - the English curriculum, including the importance of working collaboratively
>   - teaching and learning in English lessons, including performing lesson drop-ins
>   - outcomes and impact in English, including balances against assessment
> - guidance on responding to your inferences.

Pitfalls of QA

Teaching could be (and, in our opinion, should be) one of the most enviable professions in the world. When things go well, the joy of working with pupils and unlocking their potential is hard to beat. We find ourselves playing a pivotal role in enabling them to see the world differently through increasingly educated eyes. If your experience mirrors ours, you will know that every working day can be vitally important, dynamic, varied, intellectually challenging – and very, very funny.

Despite this, you will know that recruitment and retention of teachers is an increasingly difficult challenge for schools and society. The reasons for this are complex and multi-faceted, but bad QA can certainly play a part in making teaching a less attractive and less enjoyable a job. In a 2017 lecture on teacher workload, Professor Becky Allen blamed the development of an audit culture in schools for driving workload and reducing teacher happiness (Allen, 2017). In 2023, Joe Kirby outlined the negative impact QA can have on schools, teachers and leaders in a blog bluntly called *QA must die* (Kirby, 2023).

Poor QA practice not only drives teacher workload; it can also distort teacher behaviour with negative consequences for the very people it is meant to protect: the pupils we teach. Pressure to *look* good can override our inclination to *be* good (Evans, 2019, p. 89). For example, pressure to achieve high SAT outcomes can lead to teaching to the test rather than providing pupils with a well-rounded education. In the worst-case scenarios, it can lead to maladministration and cheating (Gibbons, 2020).

When QA is reduced to the two-step process of telling teachers what to do and then checking up on them, we end up with a system that values compliance over expertise (Didau, 2020). This is at odds with available evidence on effective school improvement, which points to the development of teacher expertise as a significant lever (Wiliam, 2018).

Creating a positive QA culture

In order to build an accurate picture of the strengths and weaknesses of English teaching in your school, you will need to create a culture of openness and honesty.

Robinson's work on school leadership identifies the importance of:

- using relevant knowledge and expertise to identify, explore and solve educational problems
- demonstrating competence in their job
- acting with integrity

- building relational trust with colleagues by demonstrating respect and valuing their contributions (Robinson, 2011).

Scott's book *Radical Candour* sets out a framework for creating a culture in which honest feedback – in both directions – is encouraged and embraced. This incorporates the need to offer direct challenge as necessary because of (not in spite of) care for the development of our colleagues (Scott, 2017).

If you want your colleagues to value supportive feedback, it can be helpful to model this yourself by actively and regularly seeking critique from them. This may involve explicitly asking their views on the resources you share or professional development sessions you run. Many of the examples we provide in this chapter (and, indeed, throughout this book) provide opportunities to work in collegiate manner, seeking feedback in order to keep making improvements.

It is likely that your QA will have three main focuses:

- the curriculum, including planning and resourcing
- teaching and learning within English
- pupil work and outcomes.

The rest of this chapter covers each of them in turn.

QA for curriculum planning and resourcing

Collaborative curriculum reviews

You can kickstart a positive QA culture by including your colleagues in a curriculum review. Those who teach the current planned curriculum should have vital insights into how well it is working.

Some of the best professional development sessions focus on curriculum-review activities. They can be lively and inspiring sessions in which people's passion and expertise really come to the fore. Staff also have the opportunity to reflect deeply on how their piece of the curriculum jigsaw fits into the bigger picture.

You may feel your entire English curriculum is ripe for an overhaul. In that case, you could choose to run a series of review activities working through all aspects, potentially over a full academic year. (See Chapter 13, on implementation, for guidance on leading this sort of change.) There may alternatively be one particular aspect of the curriculum, such as spelling or your reading texts, that you would like to reconsider. Either way, there are a number of approaches you could take; the table below suggests some of them. You could also use the PD suggestion at the end of this chapter to help you plan a session.

APPROACH	PROS	CONS
Emailing teachers to ask for their comments, perhaps via a short survey	The approach: • is quick and simple for you to organise • means teachers can manage when they respond and how much they wish to contribute.	The approach: • adds to colleagues' workloads • risks not getting responses from everyone • allows no opportunity for clarification or discussion.
Arranging one-to-one meetings with colleagues to discuss their ideas about the curriculum	The approach: • enables more clarification and open discussion of ideas in great detail • signals that you value colleagues' ideas highly.	The approach: • is very time consuming for you • provides scope for teachers to discuss only what they already know of the curriculum.
Asking for volunteers, or enlisting people, to work in focus groups reviewing aspects of the curriculum	The approach: • is likely to secure good buy-in from those involved • enables individuals to deepen their expertise in a particular area of the curriculum, by limiting the focus of each group.	The approach: • risks lack of buy-in from those not involved • adds to the workloads of teachers who have to contribute to multiple groups (for example in smaller schools).
Using a staff meeting to explore the curriculum	The approach: • enables rich discussion and debate across a broader team • brings together collective knowledge of the whole curriculum • builds a broader perspective by increasing teachers' awareness of what is learned in year groups other than their own.	The approach: • needs careful planning to ensure all teachers feel their time is being well used and that their input is valued • requires time to capture and follow up on ideas • runs the risk that colleagues feel disenfranchised if their ideas are not followed up.

Ongoing reviews

A large-scale review of all or part of the English curriculum may feel unnecessary, too time consuming or just not an acute enough priority at the moment. It may be that a more valid, manageable and helpful approach might be to create the conditions for ongoing feedback and review over time.

In his book *Middle Leadership Mastery*, Adam Robbins suggests keeping a 'snag list' throughout the year (Robbins, 2021). This is a live document, such as a spreadsheet, to which all teachers have access. They can be encouraged to use it to record curriculum-related issues, or areas for potential improvement, as and when they occur. These could be related, for example, to sequencing, errors in teaching materials, areas in which prior learning is not secure or helpful additional resources. Using regular reviews, you can use this list to help improve the curriculum for the following year.

QA of English teaching and learning

Using Ofsted criteria: an outdated system

It was once common practice for school leaders to use Ofsted criteria for formal lesson observations. As part of performance management, the lesson observation would be booked in advance and, on the day in question, one or two observers from the SLT would arrive to watch and take notes. The following case study provides an example of this approach.

Using Ofsted criteria in formal lesson observations

Sallie recalls being a newly qualified teacher, and having her first lesson observation booked. She really wanted to produce an outstanding lesson and spent eight hours over the weekend planning one on *Macbeth*. The lesson included:

- an 'up and out of your seats' vocabulary game
- a demonstration from an external expert in medieval weaponry and swordsmanship – with replica swords!
- multiple edited versions of a scene from the play for different attainment groups

- structured and differentiated questions for group work unpicking the meaning of the scene
- clues and glossaries dotted around the room for support
- 'sticky-note summaries' in which each pupil wrote their summary of the scene and stuck it on the door as they left.

Pupil behaviour was excellent, and the sticky notes demonstrated that learning goals had been met.

And the verdict? Sallie's lesson wasn't judged to be outstanding because the vocabulary game wasn't differentiated and the external expert talked for too long.

The above example illustrates many of the problems with this approach to QA. It is completely unrealistic for teachers to spend this long planning all of their lessons, so an observation lesson generally will not represent that teacher's usual practice or their pupils' usual experience. To save time, teachers may have developed a one-off 'showpiece' lesson ready to roll out for such observations. Observers may have realised this, disregarding the lesson to some extent to ask pupils, 'Is this what your lessons are usually like?'

Performing productive drop-ins

In recognition of how unreliable the process was, Ofsted no longer grades lesson observations. Most schools now use some form of lesson drop-in system, rather than formal observations. If you do this, it's good to frame the system as part of larger QA approaches at your school. Drop-ins will work best if they follow certain criteria.

- They should be regular. You should make them part of your school's expected culture.
- They should be brief. The goal is to gather a series of snapshots, not to make an overall judgement.
- They should be supportive in the moment. You could help pupils, assist with explaining something tricky or help to manage behaviour. You could even simply let teachers know you can bring them a drink or pick up some forgotten photocopying.
- They should be supportive between moments. You could discuss learning as you see it, and/or offer developmental feedback when appropriate.

It may be that your drop-ins are part of a school QA system, in which case you will likely have some specific school routines that you're looking to see. As a subject leader, you will also be looking to see whether the English curriculum is being taught as you expected. This has two parts to it:

- Are your colleagues teaching the curriculum you expect to be taught?
- Are they using approaches that align to those promoted by the school, and to those you have recommended?

If your school has more than one class for each year group, you may also want to look for consistency. This doesn't mean you should expect to see teachers doing exactly the same things at the same times in multiple classrooms. It means only that, overall, you want to be reassured that pupils in different classrooms are getting the same quality of teaching. If you consistently notice that one class appears to be watching videos whenever you drop in, whilst another is usually involved in class reading and discussion, you may want to explore further.

If lesson drop-ins are a new system for you or your school, it can help to explain their purpose and potential outcomes to teachers. This can be an effective way to get beyond any concerns or awkwardness that can arise. Primarily, teachers should be assured that lesson visits are used to support their development as professionals. Our QA processes and resulting actions feed into teachers' entitlement to ongoing development of them as professionals, as well as benefiting the school.

The table below outlines:

- what leaders may expect to see on lesson visits
- why they expect to see it
- how they may respond to ensure this work leads to improvements in the quality of pupil education.

It's important to note that you should recognise good practice before offering development steps. It's vital to celebrate successes, rather than focusing on only what teachers are lacking.

WHAT LEADERS EXPECT	WHY THIS IS IMPORTANT	POSSIBLE RESPONSES IF EXPECTATIONS ARE NOT MET
The classroom environment is set up to serve pupil learning.	• Every pupil should experience school as a warm, welcoming environment. • Learning should be the focus, and learning time should be optimised. • Pupils' cognitive load should be reduced as much as possible.	• Share examples of good practice in briefing/training. • Recommunicate expectations at whole-school level. • Discuss any queries with the teacher. • Agree actions for development with the teacher, and follow up on them.
The teacher is following and maintaining the school routines consistently. Either pupils are habituated to the routines or the teacher is explicitly teaching and practising them.	• Routines build physical and emotional safety for pupils. • Consistency supports colleagues. • Routines promote good pupil learning behaviours. • They prepare pupils for the next stages of education, including secondary school.	• Share examples of good practice in briefing/training. • Review your school professional development plan. • Hold bespoke training sessions for individuals or groups of teachers. • Hold a one-to-one discussion with the teacher to overcome any issues.
• The lesson is clearly identifiable as part of the curriculum plan, and the core features of effective teaching and learning are evident over time.	• Pupils are remembering more and able to do more. • Pupils are prepared for future learning.	• Share examples of good practice in briefing/training. • Invite teachers who meet expectations to coach others or contribute to whole-school professional development.

WHAT LEADERS EXPECT	WHY THIS IS IMPORTANT	POSSIBLE RESPONSES IF EXPECTATIONS ARE NOT MET
• The lesson is part of a sequence planned backwards, with a precise focus on clear learning intentions drawn from long-term curriculum plans and pupils' learning needs. • The teacher is using formative assessment to make valid inferences about the quality of pupil learning, and is responding accordingly.	• Fewer pupils need additional intervention and catch-up programmes. • Teachers need to 'backfill' learning from previous years less often. • There is marked improvement in externally validated pupil outcomes.	• Review your school professional development plan. • Hold bespoke training sessions for individuals or groups of teachers. • Hold a one-to-one discussion with the teacher to overcome any issues. • Hold discussions with school leaders, including subject leads, about ongoing reviews of processes, systems and curriculum plans.
Pupils with SEND requirements are included in whole-class teaching, and their learning needs are met.	• Pupils with SEND requirements are making progress in line with their peers. • Fewer pupils need additional support, intervention or catch-up sessions. • There is improvement in externally validated pupil outcomes for pupils with SEND requirements.	• Review the processes or referral and support from SENCo. • Invite teachers who meet expectations to coach others or contribute to whole-school professional development sessions. • Review your school professional development plan. • Hold bespoke training sessions for individuals or groups of teachers. • Hold a one-to-one discussion with the teacher to overcome any issues. • Hold discussions with school leaders, including subject leads, about ongoing reviews of processes, systems and curriculum plans.

How should an English lesson look?

Your school may promote a set of shared principles that underpin quality teaching. These could be prescribed by a non-negotiable teaching framework to which all staff must adhere. They could be based on a looser framework, for example based on the principles of cognitive science: breaking knowledge into small steps to help manage cognitive load. However, individual school subjects will always draw from distinct disciplines. How your school's principles or framework look when applied to an English lesson will be rightly different from how they look in subjects such as PE, maths or music.

As subject leader, it is therefore within your power to shape how an English lesson looks. You may find it helpful to collate a document that is separate from your school's wider guideline, summarising specifically your approach to teaching English. This can be produced collaboratively with colleagues, and then used to support QA visits to lessons and the planning of subject-specific professional development. The advantage of preparing your own document is that you can set out what works for your school within your overarching vision for the subject.

Below are examples of two different schools' approaches to reading lessons. Although they contrast with each other, both examples communicate clearly what is expected.

In practice: what you may see in reading lessons, example 1

An approach to teaching a reading lesson may look like the example below.

- **Retrieval practice**: Lessons will often, but not always, start with a quiz to check prerequisite learning and support retrieval. Questions will often be multiple choice to facilitate feedback, and answers will often be given using mini whiteboards or shows of hands.
- **Pre-teaching**: Any relevant core vocabulary (see below) or historical context will be introduced before the reading section of the lesson. This will be done through call-and-response activities with the whole class to check for understanding, followed by individual question-and-answer sessions. Care will be taken not to overload pupils with too much new knowledge at once.
- **Vocabulary**: Vocabulary instruction will cover the Tier 2 and Tier 3 vocabulary highlighted in the curriculum plan, which will be the vocabulary with the highest leverage. This vocabulary will be taught in line with our whole-school approach for teaching Star Words.

- **Reading**: All pupils will participate in reading, although most reading will be done with extensive bridging by the teacher to enliven the text. Pupils will be coached to read with expression. When reading plays, pupils will take parts. Following a first read-through, pupils will be asked to reread the text in their heads at their own pace. Reading will always be followed by preprepared questions to check for understanding.
- **Discussion and debate**: To maximise participation, all pupils will be expected to comment and share opinions on a text. The teacher will model and scaffold discussion of the text, so pupils know what to look for. Pupils will be prompted to use a 'think, pair, share' approach to develop their ideas. The teacher will ensure paired and group discussions are focused and efficient, and will cut short discussions if pupils drift in focus.
- **Assessment**: Teachers will constantly assess pupils' understanding based on quizzing, using call-and-response activities, listening to discussion and debate, using cold-call approaches, conducting question-and-answer sessions, and circulating during writing tasks. This will ensure feedback is swift and timely, and pupils are corrected immediately. Teachers will read pupils' work weekly, making notes of gaps in learning or misconceptions to be addressed. Teachers will then use these notes to plan subsequent teaching or interventions.

In practice: what you may see in reading lessons, example 2

A different approach to teaching a reading lesson may look like the example below.

- **Establishing the Big Picture**: The teacher will prioritise discussion of the text, emphasising links and connections between and within texts.
- **Focusing on detail**: The teacher will start by eliciting pupils' thoughts and feelings in relation to texts. They will then identify and explore the words, details and particular techniques that support those ideas.
- **Considering context secondarily**: The teacher will begin with pupils' responses to the text before introducing contextual information.
- **Introducing vocabulary**: Vocabulary will be explained in a light-touch way, and pupils will be encouraged to use the vocabulary in their own writing. Grammatical terms and literary techniques will be explored only when contextualised in the text being studied.

- **Questioning**: Pupils will be asked open questions that prioritise their responses to the text. A key question will be 'What is this about?'. Other common question forms will include 'What do you think of…?' and 'Why do you think…?'. Pupils will be asked what they like and don't like about any text, and will be encouraged to generate their own questions to be used by the class.
- **Reading**: The teacher will read the text with all pupils listening, in order to model expression and intonation. At points, the teacher will ask pupils to read aloud. They will ensure that all pupils have a chance to do so, with support to overcome any reluctance to speak in front of their peers.
- **Discussing and debating**: Discussion will always follow reading of the text. The teacher will pose a series of questions in a well-paced manner for pupils to explore in groups. The teacher will circulate during discussion, monitoring whether pupils are on task and intervening when necessary. Group discussion will be followed by whole-class discussion. The teacher will select pupils to share ideas, encouraging them to summarise the views of their groups and to respond to those of other groups. The teacher will guide ABC (agree, build, contradict) debates.
- **Writing responses**: Following group work, pupils will be invited to write responses to the text. At the discretion of the teacher, this may be in a series of short answer responses or a longer exploratory piece of writing.
- **Assessment**: Teachers will mark extended writing responses no more than once a week. Errors will be circled, with corrections in the margins. Pupils will be given 'Think on' questions, designed to develop their ideas in more detail. They will have the opportunity to respond to these questions at the start of the following lesson. The teacher will also hold whole-class feedback lessons that focus on modelling to improve the style of academic writing.

QA in pupil work and outcomes

Using assessments

At the end of Chapter 6, we considered how to put summative assessment to use. This involved using:

- curriculum-linked assessments to help you understand whether pupils are learning the curriculum as intended
- standardised benchmarking assessments to help you establish whether your curriculum is enabling pupils to make good progress in English.

Assessment data can form a valuable tool for QA, but it is important to remember that they have limitations. To gain a more comprehensive picture, we should triangulate assessment data with additional sources of information. This includes information from walking around the school, discussions with teachers and pupils, and reviews of pupils' work.

Work scrutiny and pupil voice

Book-looks enable you to make some useful inferences. These include:

- how much pride pupils appear to take in their English work
- to what degree the curriculum has been covered
- how consistently expectations are met across the school (such as expectations for presentation, volume and type of work)
- whether teaching appears to address misconceptions, errors and gaps
- the extent to which pupils appear to know more and/or can do more over time.

As with assessment, it is important to remember these are only inferences: we shouldn't jump to conclusions too quickly. Book-looks alone can't tell us for sure what pupils have actually learned. A perfectly presented book with no errors may be the result of over-scaffolding, for example. A messy book with lots of crossing out and reworking could indicate that a pupil is doing a great job of self-monitoring and editing their writing.

Pupils are the most significant stakeholders in schools, and listening to pupil voice can give us very useful insights into their experiences of English. Combining book-looks with pupil-voice considerations is inevitably more useful than either activity alone.

Useful questions to ask pupils about their learning could include the following.

- What are your English lessons like? What types of thing do you do? Can you show me some examples?
- What can you tell me about this work? Why is it important?
- What can you remember learning in your English lesson today/yesterday/last week?
- Can you tell me what you think makes great writing?
- What do you do if something you're reading doesn't make complete sense to you?
- What do you do if you get to a word you struggle to read?
- Can you talk to me about something in English at which you feel you've got better?
- What helps when you find English hard?
- Can you tell me about some of the things you've read in English?
- What has been your favourite text? Why is that?
- How do you feel about English as a subject? What makes you feel like that?
- How do you feel you are doing in English? What makes you feel like that?
- What in your book makes you feel most proud? Why are you particularly proud of it?

Do I need to run Ofsted-style deep dives?

Before settling on deep dives, Ofsted explored a number of methodologies for the inspection process. There is a clear rationale for the deep-dive process, which seeks to expose as much as possible about a school's curriculum within a two-day timeframe (Ofsted, 2018).

Because you are based in a school, though, you see multiple snapshots of teaching and learning every day. You participate in far more curriculum-focused conversations over time than an Ofsted inspector could ever hope to witness. If you have good planning and QA processes in place, along with a healthy culture of trust, deep dives into English shouldn't be necessary. They would also, likely, increase workload and stress for staff.

Of course, the thought of a looming Ofsted inspection can generate anxiety. It's possible that experience of deep dives could make you and your colleagues feel more prepared, but there are other actions you can take to achieve this. You could:

- engage teachers in regular reflections on the English curriculum and quality teaching of it
- support teachers in using formative assessment and responsive teaching to close learning gaps and address misconceptions
- use summative data to check the English curriculum is doing what it should over time
- talk to pupils about their learning and their work in English
- ensure pupils are regularly practising reading, with books matched to their decoding knowledge.

Everything on this list is worth doing – not for Ofsted, but because it will help you to develop your school, teachers and pupils.

Ofsted itself has blogged to advise against schools carrying out their own deep dives (Fearn & Keay, 2021). It also offers reassurance on the deep-dive process for primary subject leaders, particularly those in small primaries (Fearn & Keay, 2022). (These blogs are cited in the 'Explore further' section at the end of this chapter.)

Responding to initial inferences

It's a mistake to think that QA is merely about making observations, reaching judgements and holding people to account. An important part of the process is the discourse you will have with colleagues to understand what you have noticed. If you have concerns about something, explore what is happening with the teachers involved. That way, you give them the opportunity to solve the problem alongside you. This is more likely to secure improvement than simply telling them what they should have done.

Case study: building on inferences

Leona an English lead in a two-form-entry primary school in Kettering. Lesson visits, book-looks and pupil-voice considerations suggest to her that pupils in Year 4 aren't getting much done in their writing lessons. What work they have done does not clearly link to the objectives set out in the curriculum plan.

> Leona considers whether she should simply send the Year 4 English teacher an email. That way, she could create a record that:
>
> - highlights her concern
> - directs the teacher to the curriculum map
> - asks them to ensure they cover the necessary content by the end of term
> - lets them know she would be checking on them again in a few weeks' time.
>
> However, Leona instead decides that she will talk to the teacher. From the conversation, she discovers that the teacher lacks confidence in teaching the grammar that is part of the Year 4 writing curriculum. The curriculum map and planning available confuse them because these assume that the teacher knows more than they do. They have been trying to get around it by playing BBC Bitesize grammar videos, asking pupils to complete quizzes and then ending the lessons with short writing activities.
>
> This conversation gives Leona lot of useful information that she can use to improve English teaching in his school. The teacher not only lacks the subject knowledge to teach the lessons well; they also lack an understanding of the rationale for the English curriculum as planned. On further investigation, Leona finds that other teachers feel the same.
>
> As a result, she instigates a series of professional development sessions on the rationale for and practicalities of the school's approach to writing.

Viviane Robinson suggests having 'open to learning' conversations with teachers (Robinson, 2009). She explains that we often develop our own theories to explain teachers' behaviour, which may differ from what is actually driving their actions. If there is a mismatch between our theories and the teachers' challenges, we end up attempting to solve the wrong problems. Robinson's recommendation offers us a route to engage with teachers' beliefs and to work with them to agree on solutions. In this way, we will develop the trust that is key to leading school improvement.

Chapter summary

- Approaches to QA should be nuanced, so *looking* good doesn't override *being* good.
- It is important to create a positive two-way QA culture.
- Performing curriculum reviews collaboratively will be both productive and engaging.
- Lesson drop-ins are more constructive than formal lesson observations.
- It's helpful to formulate and share a list of criteria to check during lesson drop-ins.
- Constructing lesson plans for English should respect, but needn't be limited by, whole-school frameworks and principles.
- Inferences based on assessments should be balanced with work scrutiny and pupil voice.
- We shouldn't assume we understand teachers' challenges without consulting them.

Questions for reflection

- What are our current QA processes for English? Are they understood well by all teaching staff?
- Do our processes support us to make valid inferences about the quality of the English curriculum and English teaching?
- Are your QA systems driving any unnecessary workload? What can I do about this?
- Are there any changes or improvements I would like to make?
- How might I go about doing this? What support do I need?

Example PD session: collaboratively reviewing the curriculum

You could conduct a PD session to review your English curriculum with colleagues as follows:

TIMING SUGGESTION	SESSION GUIDANCE
Before the session	Prepare copies of English planning overviews and medium-term plans for each year group place or display them side by side.
10 minutes	<ul><li>Explain what you will be doing and why.</li><li>Remind everyone of your school curriculum ethos.</li><li>Explore any concepts or language with which colleagues may be unfamiliar, ensuring a shared understanding.</li></ul>For example: I've been looking forward to beginning this comprehensive review of our English curriculum with you. The primary goal of the review is simple: does our curriculum capture our ambitions for pupils' capabilities? Your input and expertise will be invaluable. We know our school ethos for curriculums is that knowledge is valued, specified, well-sequenced and taught to be remembered. Let's start by digging into that.
40 minutes	Break up this time by providing focal points for conversations. Teachers should discuss points whilst referring to the planning. For example:<ul><li>Are we teaching the most important things? Is anything missing?</li><li>Is there a good model for progression? Does learning build through this curriculum? Are there any big gaps or unintentional repetition?</li><li>Do you question the value of any knowledge being taught?</li><li>Are we happy with the range of fiction, poems and plays? Are we including enough quality non-fiction?</li><li>Does this plan give the opportunity for mastery of writing?</li><li>Does the plan reflect what we are actually teaching? Do you feel surprised that pupils are expected to have knowledge of anything you don't feel pupils have learned?</li><li>Is there anything you feel is in the wrong place? Why is that?</li></ul>

TIMING SUGGESTION	SESSION GUIDANCE
10 minutes	- Summarise key points to take away and check all are in agreement. - Make any next steps clear. For example: We've agreed we don't feel there is enough poetry in the curriculum. Anna will email me some great suggestions – if you think of any more, let me know. I'll share a new curriculum plan with you by the end of term, so you can let me know what you think.

Explore further

- *Classroom observation: it's harder than you think* (2014) by Rob Coe: https://www.cem.org/blog/classroom-observation
- *Intelligent Accountability: Creating the Conditions for Teachers to Thrive* (2020) by David Didau
- Ofsted's *Curriculum: keeping it simple* (2021) by Heather Fearn and Jonathan Keay: https://educationinspection.blog.gov.uk/2021/12/08/curriculum-keeping-it-simple/
- Ofsted's *What to expect on a primary deep dive* (2022) by Heather Fearn and Jonathan Keay: https://educationinspection.blog.gov.uk/2022/02/02/what-to-expect-on-a-primary-deep-dive-some-guidance-for-subject-leaders/
- *Successful Difficult Conversations in School* (2018) by Sonia Gill
- *Background Paper Introduction to Open-to-learning Conversations* by Viviane M. J. Robinson: https://www.researchgate.net/publication/267411000_Open-to-learning_Conversations_Background_Paper_Introduction_to_Open-to-learning_Conversations
- *Student-Centred Leadership* (2011) by Viviane M. J. Robinson
- *Radical Candour* (2017) by Kim Scott

13 Implementing change

As English lead, you will almost certainly be asked to write an action plan each year for strategic development of the subject. Your plan is likely to:

- identify the key priorities
- set timescales for completing the actions
- include criteria for judging whether each priority has been implemented successfully.

Three priorities are plenty, in our experience, in order that you can devote sufficient time and resources to each. Further, some priorities may take more than one year to implement, and you may need to scope out a three-year plan that feeds into your yearly plan. It is therefore important to consider your priorities very carefully.

Considering implementation as a system of small steps can be supportive. This chapter is intended to serve as a guide on how to do this, following the EEF guidance on stages of implementation. We'll go through each of the suggested stages step by step, providing a case study for each stage.

Planning for success

To move your subject forwards, your priorities should ultimately improve outcomes for all pupils. There are many options you could choose to achieve this, and the following are some of the most common.

- Vocabulary: building vocabulary knowledge and use through implicit and explicit instruction
- Reading fluency: developing reading that is accurate, automatic and well intoned
- Reading interest: promoting independent reading for pleasure and information

- Sentence structure: building familiarity with and use of a range of sentence forms
- Handwriting: developing legibility and fluency
- Spelling: improving ability to apply code knowledge and recognise spelling patterns
- Curriculum development: clarifying core knowledge and granular steps for each year group
- Resourcing: providing materials needed for the development of both pupils' and teachers' knowledge

Your action plan, however, is only the start of this work: it is its implementation that matters. Many a well-intentioned plan has failed to move a subject forwards, and this could happen for a variety of reasons.

Coe (2013) identifies a wide array of reasons why school-improvement strategies may not work, including a lack of capacity or resources. Robinson (2018) also identifies that many new strategies introduced increase demands on teachers, so it's important we spend enough time exploring the issues and possible solutions before introducing them. Other common reasons include the ones below – and we are sure school leaders will be able to add more.

- It takes longer than one year to implement and embed sustained change.
- Not enough time has been taken to identify what is actually required for the plan to be impactful.
- The leader is trying to implement too many things at the same time.
- The priorities do not align with those of the whole-school development plan.
- Not enough time has been devoted to knowledge-building with teachers, meaning they are not confident implementing the changes.
- The plan is too wide-ranging, and the success criteria are not sufficiently detailed for staff to identify impact.
- The priorities are generic issues that do not consider the school's context.

> **Tips for subject leaders: creating implementation plans**
>
> You could draw on the following ideas when creating your implementation plan.
>
> - Consider expert knowledge. We hope this book will provide a useful starting point for you to build your knowledge and explore further resources.
> - Collect the right data. Spend time collecting and triangulating data to ensure you have identified productive key priorities. All too often, solutions are sought for symptoms rather than their causes.
> - Consider a reductive structure rather than an additive one. Do you need to introduce a new approach, or do you need to continue to refine and embed what is already in place?

The EEF guide to implementation

There are no hard-and-fast rules for ensuring successful implementation of a new strategy, but taking a deliberate and structured approach to how the strategy is introduced and applied can have a significant impact on the likelihood of its success (Sharples et al., 2024).

The EEF's Guide to Implementation (Sharples et al., 2024) provides a useful framework for planning the implementation of priorities. The guidance segments this process into four key stages of successful implementation, each incorporating a series of steps. They are laid out in summary below.

EXPLORE
Step 1: Identify a priority.
Step 2: Make evidence-informed decisions about a solution to implement.
Step 3: Examine the solution's fit and feasibility regarding your context.
PREPARE
Step 4: Develop a clear, logical and well-specified implementation plan.
Step 5: Assess your school's readiness to deliver the implementation plan.

DELIVER
Step 6: Adopt a flexible and motivating leadership approach.
Step 7: Provide comprehensive follow-on support.
Step 8: Use implementation data actively, to tailor and improve the approach.
SUSTAIN
Step 9: Regularly review progress, and decide how to proceed.
Step 10: Maintain ongoing support and monitoring.

As we look at each phase, we will use a case study to help us consider how this may look in practice.

1. The 'Explore' phase

At this first phase, you should:

1. identify a priority in response to assessment data, lesson visits, pupil discussions and/or book-looks

2. ensure that the strategy you propose is informed by evidence

3. consider whether it is right for your setting and feasible to implement. If it is introducing a significant change, such as a new approach to teaching reading, you will need to identify whether there are any other significant changes planned in your school. The introduction of, for example, a new maths scheme of work will mean you may want to consider delaying the implementation. This should be a discussion you hold with your headteacher.

It can be tempting to make knee-jerk decisions based on statutory assessments. Indeed (as discussed in Chapter 7, on reading after EYFS), low scores in reading comprehension assessments can lead to a focus on practising reading comprehension questions, particularly using inference. These can then take precedence over teaching pupils the core skills of reading and analysing texts. Equally, poor spelling at the end of Key Stage 2 could result in plans to spend significant time practising spellings in Year 6; the issue, however, more likely originated in earlier stages. In that example, time instead should be spent looking at the whole-school approach to teaching spelling (as discussed in Chapter 10, on spelling).

When selecting criteria for action-plan priorities, we recommend considering the following.

- Are all strands of your English curriculum sufficiently detailed to clarify the core knowledge for all pupils in all year groups?
- Do you use detailed curriculum plans to support assessment?
  - How are formative and summative assessments balanced?
  - Are pupil-voice discussions and book-looks based on the core knowledge taught for that year group?
- Are there particular groups of pupils or curriculum areas that show less progress than others?
- Do all staff members have the necessary subject knowledge to teach your curriculum effectively?

During the 'Explore' phase, asking lots of questions and being curious will support you to identify development needs. (You could see Chapter 12, on QA practices, for further guidance on collecting and using data.)

The following table summarises types of data and next steps you could consider during this phase.

TYPES OF DATA	NEXT STEPS
- Lesson drop-ins - Planning reviews - Pupil-voice discussions - Book-looks - Informal conversations with colleagues - Resource audits - Data from formative and summative assessments	- Exploring hunches by triangulating data - Asking more questions - Considering curriculum adjustments - Considering professional development provision for you and your teaching staff - Reviewing planning - Reviewing the availability of resources

Case study: running the 'Explore' phase

1: Identify a priority
- Sunil is an English subject lead at a four-form-entry primary school in Aberystwyth. He wants to improve the percentage of pupils achieving age-related expectations (ARE) in reading at the end of KS2.
- Sunil identifies that, over the last year, KS2 reading results are significantly below the national average for 45% of his pupils from lower socio-economic backgrounds.
- This is not dissimilar from the previous year's results, so he knows the problem is unlikely to be specific to one cohort.
- He explores further, and identifies that:
  - reading lessons for pupils in Years 2 to 6 consist of reading extracts and answering comprehension questions
  - although some teachers identify and teach Tier 2 vocabulary implicitly, vocabulary is not taught explicitly, meaning pupils often do not fully understand what they were reading
  - pupils working below ARE attend reading intervention sessions with teaching assistants in place of the class reading lessons.

2: Make evidence-informed decisions about a solution to implement
- Sunil knows from his reading that comprehension is strongly reliant on vocabulary and background knowledge. He also knows that reading interventions should take place in addition to class reading lessons, not instead of them.
- He refers to the EEF guidance on improving literacy at KS1 and KS2, which recommends teaching new words explicitly, providing repeated exposure to them and ensuring opportunities for pupils to use them.
- He also refers to other sources, including research on vocabulary acquisition.

> **3: Examine the solution's fit and feasibility regarding your context**
> - Sunil decides that a priority in his action plan will be for pupils to read complete texts, and for teachers to establish all pupils have understood the meaning of what they've read before asking analysis questions.
> - Sunil recognises that this will be a big shift in teaching approach for teachers. He knows it will be a big project, and will need to be broken into stages.
> - Sunil decides to run PD sessions that focus on the importance of vocabulary instruction and how this should look in reading lessons. He believes that this is likely to have the most impact on reading comprehension for all pupils, and particularly those from lower socio-economic backgrounds.

2. The 'Prepare' phase

At the prepare phase, you will need to plot your entire implementation journey. This will include consideration of:

- **why** the change is taking place
- **what** the strategy entails: its core components
- **how** it will be implemented, including PD provision, resources and timescales
- **how well** implementation may go: ways to check progress
- **where** the change should take your staff and pupils: its intended outcomes.

When new ways of working are being learned, new behaviours need to be adopted and old habits set aside. This can be hard for experienced staff, so it is important that you bring them along with you on the journey. Sharing the rationale and including them in the 'Prepare' phase of your implementation plan will be both productive and companionable.

Case study: running the 'Prepare' phase

4: Develop a clear, logical and well-specified implementation plan
- Sunil writes his implementation plan and talks it through with his headteacher. It:
  - defines the problem and the rationale
  - identifies the active ingredients for vocabulary instruction
  - identifies the PD sessions that will be required
  - identifies implementation strategies, including the rationale for providing vocabulary instruction, modelling lessons, sharing lesson plans, team-teaching and coaching.
- After agreeing the priority with his headteacher, Sunil plans how he will evaluate the implementation, including lesson drop-ins and being responsive to individual needs.
- He plans his outcome evaluation including short-, medium- and long-term criteria.
  - In the short term, staff will be:
- enthusiastic about the new approach to vocabulary instruction
- able to engage with implementation strategies fully
- clear about expectations
- aware of the support available
- engaged in PD that is aligned to core components.
  - In the medium term, staff will:
- Use new approaches to vocabulary instruction in their lessons
- feel that the new approach is supporting pupils who are reading below ARE
- report that pupils have more confidence when reading and discussing class texts.
  - In the long term:
- vocabulary instruction will be embedded in all classes
- systems and structures will be in place to train new staff and refresh existing practices
- pupils will be using taught vocabulary when discussing their texts.

5: Assess your school's readiness to deliver the implementation plan
- Sunil identifies teachers who already teach vocabulary implicitly in their reading lessons and are likely to welcome the change. He also identifies teachers who might need extra support.
- Sunil speaks to his headteacher about the proposed PD programme and other school priorities. Together, they map out when the sessions will take place. These include time for teachers to plan together, with support from Sunil.

3. The 'Deliver' phase

The 'Deliver' phase involves enabling ongoing improvement as you implement a new strategy. It is important to create a culture in which lesson drop-ins are seen as opportunities for staff to showcase what is going well and ask for support where it's not. Implementation will be more likely to succeed in that context than when drop-ins feel like they are just about monitoring.

Providing timely prompts and reminders can help teachers feel connected to a strategy, maintain commitment and improve fidelity. Revisiting the core components of your new approach to vocabulary instruction, for example, will help to embed it. It is key that you model new techniques, and provide regular opportunities for teachers to rehearse instruction and identify vocabulary for their lessons. It is also important that you encourage teachers to discuss problems, share insights and give you feedback. You could conduct short surveys as well as having open discussions during this phase, to tease out barriers to development.

As the project is implemented, monitoring will almost certainly reveal issues and setbacks. You are likely to have anticipated and planned for some of them, but others may not have been foreseen. Building in flexibility can help to reduce barriers, allowing you to give more-tailored support to individuals or groups. Equally, you could spotlight colleagues who have picked up the new approach more quickly: this can provide opportunities for those colleagues to model good practice for their peers.

Case study: running the 'Deliver' phase

6: Adopt a flexible and motivating leadership approach
- Having agreed the PD programme with his headteacher, Sunil holds an initial session to familiarise his colleagues with his implementation plan.
- He begins by clearly explaining the rationale for the change. He explains what he has learned from school data and research evidence, and emphasises the plan's particular benefits for pupils from lower socio-economic backgrounds.
- He acknowledges that implementing a change can feel challenging at first, and reassure teachers that there will be plenty of training and support along the way. He provides planning examples and a checklist of active ingredients to support planning.
- Sunil ensures he remains visible and available before, during and at the end of the school day as much as possible. He regularly checks in with teachers to offer support and encouragement, and invites them to watch him teach vocabulary lessons. He also records some of his lessons for teachers to watch in PD sessions.
- Sunil works collaboratively with his headteacher to identify and spotlight staff teaching vocabulary explicitly, and praises them publicly.

7: Provide comprehensive follow-on support
- Sunil works with teachers to plan their vocabulary lessons.
- He identifies teachers who are adopting the new approach successfully, and pairs them with teachers who will benefit from having planning partners.
- Sunil continues to offer team-teach sessions, and to invite colleagues to watch him teach.

8: Use implementation data actively, to tailor and improve the approach
- Through his lesson drop-ins, discussions with staff, and observations from his headteacher and wider leadership team, Sunil identifies that one year-group team is not planning explicit vocabulary instruction that includes all the active ingredients.
- After discussion with his headteacher, he works with the team to unpick this. He learns that the year-group leader missed the initial PD session in which Sunil shared the rationale and evidence base for his plan. As a result, she has not fully bought in to the change and has not made time for vocabulary instruction in her weekly planning meetings.
- Sunil works with the year-group leader in the first instance, and then joins the year-group team meetings for a couple of weeks. In this way, he can support teachers as they learn to include all the active ingredients for vocabulary instruction in their planning.
- He checks in with the team over the following weeks and tailors further support for individuals as necessary.

4. The 'Sustain' phase

The 'Sustain' phase will help to ensure your new approach remains embedded beyond its initial delivery. Revisiting and adapting your plan, refreshing professional development provisions and sharing improved outcomes are all key contributing factors. It is also constructive to revisit and refine your checklist of active ingredients, share planning examples and ensure your approach is part of the induction process for new staff members.

If you have introduced a new phonics programme, for example, you can maintain its profile and fidelity by holding regular 5–10-minute phonics refresher sessions for teachers, and parent workshops throughout the year.

Case study: running the 'Sustain' phase

9: Regularly review progress, and decide how to proceed
- At the end of the second term of implementation, Sunil conducts a full review of both the new process and its outcome data.
- He asks:
  - Are teachers routinely including vocabulary instruction in reading lessons?
  - Are pupils reading and comprehending challenging texts?
  - Are pupils using taught Tier 2 and Tier 3 vocabulary when discussing texts?
  - Can we observe rapid progress in pupils who were working below ARE?
  - Are reading-fluency assessments showing a decrease in the gap between pupils from different socio-economic backgrounds?
- Sunil decided to continue with the strategy, but also to return to Step 1 and gather more data to decide the next steps.

10: Maintain ongoing support and monitoring.
- To monitor implementation and impact, Sunil continues to conduct lesson drop-ins and to have conversations with pupils about the vocabulary they are learning in English lessons.
- He ensures that new staff members received training on vocabulary instruction as part of their induction to the school.
- Sunil regularly reported on the progress of the strategy to the school leadership team, maintaining their support for the ongoing initiative.
- He establishes that teachers could see the impact of vocabulary instruction in whole-class reading lessons. After this success, he begins to develop PD programmes on the other aspects of reading instruction that he'd hoped to address in addition.

An implementation plan

There is not one agreed way to lay out an implementation plan. However, to ensure successful implementation, it is important to set a plan and work through it methodically. Many schools use a simple action plan proforma.

The case study below shows how an English lead identified a school priority around reading fluency and identified key actions on the school's action plan proforma. She used her knowledge of the EEF implementation guidance to ensure the priority was most likely to embed and sustain over time.

Case study: improving reading fluency

Tanika is English lead in a large junior school in Leicester. She introduced reading-fluency lessons for all year groups at the beginning of the last academic year, and saw an increase in reading-fluency scores for most pupils in the spring term. (See Chapter 6 and 7, on reading, for information on the importance of fluency for improving all pupils' reading progress.)

However, when she analyses the reading-fluency scores in the summer term, she finds that this progress has not been not maintained. This is particularly true for KS2 pupils from lower socio-economic backgrounds. The deputy headteacher (DHT) shares with her that he is not seeing reading-fluency sessions regularly in all classes during his drop-ins. Tanika is also mindful that four new teachers will be joining the school in September.

Together, Tanika and the deputy head agree that reading fluency should continue to be an English priority for the coming academic year. Below is the section of the action plan that Tanika completes to address reading fluency.

PRIORITY: 95% OF PUPILS TO BE 'GREEN' IN THEIR TERMLY FLUENCY ASSESSMENTS		
ACTIONS	LEADER	TIME SCALES
As in-service training (INSET), hold Professional development sessions for all staff on: • conceptual underpinnings • routines for whole-class fluency lessons.	English subject leader (ESL)	October

PRIORITY: 95% OF PUPILS TO BE 'GREEN' IN THEIR TERMLY FLUENCY ASSESSMENTS		
As INSET, hold professional development sessions for teachers on: • planning fluency lessons • deliberate practice • keep-up and catch-up interventions.	ESL	October
Hold professional development sessions on: • improving intonation, automaticity and pace • timetabling and organisation for catch-up interventions.	ESL and DHT	October (introduction) and ongoing (monitoring and adjusting)
Hold professional development sessions: • spotlighting embedded practice • unpicking filmed lessons.	ESL	January
Monitor pupils undertaking catch-up interventions to ensure impact, baselines and daily timetabling.	ESL and DHT	October and ongoing
Hold professional development sessions with support staff on leading catch-up interventions.	ESL	November and ongoing
Review progress, half-termly for pupils in catch-up interventions and termly for core.	ESL	January and ongoing

Chapter summary

- Many implementation plans do not work because not enough time is spent exploring the problem and planning how to address it.
- The EEF's Guide to Implementation can help us to plan using the four preparation and planning phases it specifies:

- Explore: After identifying a priority, you should consider possible solutions in the light of expert research, school data and your school's context.
- Prepare: Your plan should be carefully sequenced, and consider the 'why', 'what' and 'how' of the change being promoted. Buy-in from teachers is vital.
- Deliver: You should action new approaches to teaching through comprehensive but flexible PD training, follow-up support and responsive feedback.
- Sustain: It is important to review progress and continue monitoring to inform improvements to the approach.

Questions for reflection

- How do I identify action-plan priorities? What data do I collect? How do I involve others in your decisions?
- How do I plan PD sessions to support the implementation of my priorities? What conversations do I need to have with our school leadership team to support me with this?
- Do I need to consider changes to our current monitoring systems? Whom will I consult? What further information do I need?
- Are there some priorities that have not embedded as I anticipated? Can I identify the reasons for this? What steps do I need to take now?

Explore further

- The EEF's *A School's Guide to Implementation* (2024) by J. Sharples, J. Eaton and J. Boughelaf: https://educationendowmentfoundation.org.uk/education-evidence/guidance-reports/implementation
- The Institute for Effective Education's *What are active ingredients?* (2020) by J. Haslam
- *Reduce Change to Increase Improvement* (2018) by V. Robinson

Bibliography

Alexander, R. (2018), 'Developing dialogic teaching: Genesis, process, trial'. *Research Papers in Education*, 33(5), 561–598.

Alexander, R. (2020), *A Dialogic Teaching Companion*. Abingdon: Routledge.

Allen, R. (2017), 'Making teaching a job worth doing (again)'. *Rebecca Allen*, https://rebeccaallen.co.uk/wp-content/uploads/2010/07/2017-11-becky-allen-on-workload.pdf

Amendum, S. J., Conradi, K., & Hiebert, E. (2017), 'Does text complexity matter in the elementary grades? A reserach synthesis of text difficulty and elementary student's reading fluency and comprehension'. *Educational Pscychology Review*, 30, 121–151.

Andrews, R., Beverton, S., Locke, T., Low, G., Robinson, A., Torgerson, C., & Zhu, D. (2004), 'The effect of grammar teaching (syntax) in English on 5 to 16 year olds' accuracy and quality in written composition'. *Research Evidence in Education Library*. London: EPPI Centre, Social Science Research Unit, Institute of Education.

Ashbee, R. (2021), *Curriculum: Theory, culture and the subject specialisms*. Abingdon: Routledge.

Baddeley, A. D., & Hitch, G. (1974), 'Working Memory'. *Psychology of Learning and Motivation*, 8, 47–899.

Bandura, A. (1997), *Self-Efficacy: The exercise of control*. New York: W.H. Freeman and Company.

Barbash, S. (2012), *Clear Teaching: With Direct Instruction, Siegfried Engelmann Discovered a Better Way of Teaching*. Washington, DC: Education Consumers Foundation.

Barker, J., & Rees, T. (2020), 'Developing School Leadership', in Lock, S. (ed) *The ResearchEd Guide to Leadership*. Woodbridge: John Catt.

Beck, I. L., McKeown, M. G., & Omanson, R. C. (1987), 'The effects and uses of diverse vocabulary instructional techniques', in McKeown, M. G. & Curtis, M.E. *The nature of vocabulary acquisition*. London: Psychology Press, pp. 147–163.

Beck, I.L., McKeown, M.G., & Kucan, L. (2013), *Bringing Words to Life*. New York: Guildford.

Bilton, C. and Duff, A. (2021), *Improving Literacy in Key Stage 2 Guidance* Report (2nd edition). London: Education Endowment Foundation.

Bilton, C. and Tillotson, S. (2021a), *Improving Literacy in Key Stage 1* Guidance Report (2nd edition). London: Education Endowment Foundation.

Beringer, V. W., Vaughan, K., Curtin, G., & Graham, S. (2002), 'Teaching Spelling and Composition Alone and Together: Implications for the Simple View of Writing'. *Journal of Educational Psychology*, 94(2), 291–304.

Black, P., Harrison, C., Marshall, B., & Wiliam, D. (2004), 'Working inside the Black Box: Assessment for Learning in the Classroom', *Phi Delta Kappan* 86(1), 8–21.

Boulton, K. (2019), 'What was Project Follow Through?' in Boxer, A. (ed), *The researchED guide to Explicit and Direct Instruction*. Woodbridge: John Catt, pp. 15–19.

Boxer, A. (ed) (2019), *The researchED Guide to Explicit and Direct Instruction*. Woodbridge: John Catt.

Byrnes, J. P., & Wasick, B. A. (2009), *Language and Literacy Development: What Educators Need To Know*. New York: Guildford.

Castles, A., Rastle, K., & Nation, K. (2018), 'Ending the reading wars: Reading acquisition from novice to expert'. *Psychological Science in Public Interest*, 19(1), 5–51.

Catts, H. W. (2018), 'The Simple View of Reading: Advancements and False Impressions'. *Remedial and Special Education*, 39(5), 317–323.

Chall, J. S. (1983), *Stages of Reading Development*. New York: McGraw-Hill.

Chall, J. S., & Jacobs, V. A. (2003), Poor children's fourth-grade slump. *American Educator*, 27, 14–15.

Chard, D. J., Vaugh, S., & Tyler, B. J. (2002), 'A synthesis of research on effective interventions for building reading fluency with elementary students with learning disabilities'. *Journal of Learning Disabilities*, 35(5), 386–406.

Chomsky, N. (1957), *Syntactic Structures*. The Hague: Mouton and Co.

Chomsky, N. (1965), *Aspects of the Theory of Syntax*. Cambridge, MA: MIT Press.

Christodoulou, D. (2014), *Seven Myths About Education*. Abingdon: Routledge.

Christodoulou, D. (2016), *Making Good Progress? The future of assessment for learning*. Oxford: Oxford University Press.

Clark, C., & Rumbold, K. (2006), *Reading for Pleasure: A Research Overview*. London: The National Literacy Trust.

Clark, C., & De Zoysa, S. (2011), *Mapping the interrelationships of reading enjoyment, attitudes, behaviour and attainment. An exploratory investigation*. London: The National Literary Trust.

Coe, R. (2013), *Improving Education: A triumph of hope over experience*. Gateshead: Centre for Evaluation and Monitoring.

Coe, R. (2014), 'Classroom observation: it's harder than you think'. *Cambridge University Press Centre for Evaluation and Monitoring Blog*, https://www.cem.org/blog/classroom-observation.

Crystal, D. (2005), *The Stories of English*. London: Penguin.

Crystal, D. (2018), *The Cambridge Encyclopedia of the English Language*. Cambridge: Cambridge University Press.

Cunningham, A., & Stanovich, K. (1988), 'What reading does for the mind'. *American Educator*, 22(1 and 2), 8–15.

De Bruyckere, P., Kirschner, P. A. & Hulshof, C. D. (2015). *Urban Myths about Learning and Education*. Netherlands: Academic Press.

Dennis, D. (2020), 'Prioritising teaching children to write' in Lock, S. *The ResearchEd Guide to Leadership*. Woodbridge: John Catt, pp. 173–184.

Department for Education (DfE) (2013), *The National Curriculum for England: Key Stages 1 and 2 Framework Document*. London: Department for Education.

Department for Education (DfE) (2013), *English Programmes of Study: Key Stages 1 and 2*. London: Department for Education.

Department for Education (DfE) (2023), *The Reading Framework*. London: Department for Education

Department for Education (DfE) (2023), *Validation of systematic synthetic phonics programmes: supporting documentaion*. London: Department for Education.

Department for Education (DfE) (2025), *Phonics screening check: information for parents*. London: Department for Education.

Didau, D. (2020), *Intelligent Accountability: creating the conditions for teachers to thrive*. Woodbridge: John Catt.

Didau, D. (2021), *Making Meaning in English: Exploring the role of knowledge in the English curriculum*. Abingdon: Routledge.

Didau, D., Blackburn, D., Levins, E., Moloney, K., Pinkstone, T., Rose, A. and Hibbert, J. (2024), *Bringing the English Curriculum to Life*. Abingdon: Routledge.

Durand, F., Lawson, H., Wilcox, K., & Schiller, K. (2016), 'The Role of District Office Leaders in the Adoption and Implementation of the Common Core State Standards in Elementary Schools'. *Educational Administration Quarterly*, 52(1), pp. 45–74.

Education Endowment Foundation (EEF) (2018), *Preparing for Literacy* : Improving Communication, Language and Literacy in the Early Years. London: Education Endowment Foundation.

Education Endowment Foundation (EEF) (2021), *Teaching and Learning Toolkit: Metacognition and self-regulation*. London: Education Endowment Foundation https://educationendowmentfoundation.org.uk/education-evidence/teaching-learning-toolkit/metacognition-and-self-regulation.

Ehri, L. C. (1995), 'Phases of development in learning to read words by sight'. *Journal of Research in Reading*, 2, 116–125.

Evans, M. (2019), *Leaders with Substance*. Woodbridge: John Catt.

Fearn, H., & Keay, J. (2021), 'Curriculum: keeping it simple', *Ofsted blog*, https://educationinspection.blog.gov.uk/2021/12/08/curriculum-keeping-it-simple/.

Fearn, H., & Keay, J. (2022), 'What to expect on a primary deep dive – some guidance for subject leaders', *Ofsted blog*, https://educationinspection.blog.gov.uk/2022/02/02/what-to-expect-on-a-primary-deep-dive-some-guidance-for-subject-leaders/

Fernald, A., Marchman, V. A., & Weisleder, A. (2013), 'SES Differences in Language Processing Skill and Vocabulary Are Evident at 18 Months'. *Developmental Science*, 16(2), 234–48.

Fletcher-Wood, H. (2018), *Responsive Teaching: Cognitive Science and Formative Assessment in Practice*. Abingdon: Routledge.

Gibbons, A. (2020), 'Analysis: How common is SATs maladministration?' *Tes Magazine*, https://www.tes.com/magazine/archive/analysis-how-common-sats-maladministration

Gill, S. (2018), *Successful Difficult Conversations in School: Improve your team's performance, behaviour and attitude with kindness and success*. Woodbridge: John Catt.

GL Assessment (2020), *Read All About It: Why reading is key to GCSE success*. London: GL Assessment.

Glenberg, A. M., Meyer, M., & Lindem, K. (1987), 'Mental models contribute to foregrounding during text comprehension'. *Journal of Memory and Language*, 26(1), 69–83.

Gough, P. B., & Hillinger, M. L. (1980), 'Learning to read: An unnatural act'. *Bulletin of the Orton Society*, 179–196.

Graham, S., & Perin, D. (2007), *Writing Next: Effective Strategies to Improve Writing of Adolescents in Middle and High Schools*. New York: Carnegie.

Gruhn, S., Segers, E., & Verhoeven, L. (2019), 'The Efficiency of Briefly Presenting Word Forms in Computerised Repeated Spelling Training'. *Reading and Writing Quarterly*, 35(3), 225–242.

Harley, J. (2020), *The Oxford Language Report*. Oxford: Oxford University Press.

Hart, B., & Risley, T. R. (1995), *Meaningful differences in the everyday experience of young American children*. Baltimore, MD: Brookes Publishing Company.

Higgins, S., Henderson, P., Martell, T., Sharples, J. and Waugh, D. (2020), *Improving Literacy in Key Stage 1 Guidance Report* (1st edition). London: Education Endowment Foundation.

Hart, B., & Risley, T. (2003), 'The Early Catastrophe - The 30 Million Word Gap by Age 3'. *American Educator*, 27, 4–9.

Hirsch, J. E. D. (2013), 'A Wealth of Words'. *City Journal*, https://www.city-journal.org/article/a-wealth-of-words

Hochman, J.C. and Wexler, N. with Maloney, K (2017), *The Writing Revolution*. Hoboken, NJ: Jossey-Bass.

Hoover, W. A. and Gough, P. B. (1990), 'The simple view of reading'. *Reading and Writing* 2(2):127–160.

Hudson, R. F., Lane, H. B., & Pullen, P. C. (2005), 'Reading fluency assessment and instruction: What, why, and how?' *The Reading Teacher*, 58(8), 702–714.

Jones, S., Myhill, D., & Bailey, T. (2012), 'Grammar for writing? An investigation of the effects of contextualised grammar teaching on student's writing'. *Reading and Writing*, 26, 10.

Kennedy, M. (2016), 'Parsing the practice of teaching'. *Journal of Teacher Education*, 6–17.

Kilpatrick, D., & O'Brien, S. (2019), 'Effective prevention and intervention for word-level reading difficulties' in Kilpatrick, D. Joshi, R. M and Wagner, R. K. (eds), *Reading Development Difficulties*. Schweiz: Springer International Publishing.

Kintsch, W. (1988), 'The role of knowledge in discourse comprehension: A construction-integration model'. *Psychological Review*, 95(2).

Kirby, J. (2023), 'QA Must Die'. *Joe-kirby.com*, https://joe-kirby.com/2023/03/18/qa-must-die/

Kirschner, P. A., & Hendrick, C. (2020), *How Learning Happens Seminal Works in Educational Psychology and What They Mean in Practice*. Abingdon: Routledge.

Koretz, D. (2008), *Measuring Up: What Educational Testing Really Tells Us*. Cambridge, MA: Harvard University Press.

Korochkina, M., Marelli, M., Brysbaert, M., & Rastle, K. (2024), 'The Children and Young People's Books Lexicon (CYP-LEX): A large-scale lexical database of books read by children and young people in the United Kingdom'. *Quarterly Journal of Experimental Psychology*, 77(12), 2418–2438.

Lavan, G., & Talcott, J. B. (2020), 'What Works for Literacy Difficulties? Grammar For Writing'. *The School Psychology Service*, https://www.theschoolpsychologyservice.com/what-works/grammarforwriting/

Law, J., Charlton, J., Dockrell, J., Gascoigne, M., McKean, C., & Theakston, A. (2017), *Early Language Development: Needs, provision, and intervention for preschool children from socio-economically disadvantage backgrounds: A Report for the Education Endowment Foundation*. London: Education Endowment Foundation and Public Health England.

Lemov, D., Driggs, C., & Woolway, E. (2016), *Reading Reconsidered: A Practical Guide for Rigorous Literacy Instruction*. San Francisco: Jossey-Bass.

Mannion, J. (2023), 'The Transformative Power of Oracy'. *Oracy Cambridge*, https://oracycambridge.org/oracy-at-the-heart-of-the-curriculum/

McCrea, P. (2020), *Motivated Teaching*. North Charleston, SC: CreateSpace Independent Publishing Platform.

McCrum, W., Macneil, R., & Cran, R. (1986), *The Story of English*. London: Faber and Faber.

McGinlay, M. (2022), 'Implementing the Great Teaching Toolkit'. *Evidence Based Education*, https://evidencebased.education/implementing-the-great-teaching-toolkit/

McGuinness, D. (2006), *Early Reading Instruction*. Cambridge, MA: MIT Press.

Mercer, N. (1995), *The guided construction of knowledge: Talk amongst teachers and learners*. Clevedon: Multilingual Matters.

Mercer, N., Wegerif, R., & Major, L. (eds) (2019), *The Routledge International Handbook of Research on Dialogic Education*. Abingdon: Routledge.

National Reading Panel (U.S.), (2000), *Report of the National Reading Panel: Teaching children to read: an evidence-based assessment of the scientific research literature on reading and its implications for reading instruction*. Rockville, MD: National Institute of Child Health and Human Development.

Oakhill, J., Cain, K., & Elbro, C. (2014), *Understanding and Teaching Reading Comprehension: A Handbook*. Abingdon: Routledge.

Ofsted (2018), 'An investigation into how to assess the quality of education through curriculum intent, implementation and impact'. *Ofsted*, https://www.gov.uk/government/publications/curriculum-research-assessing-intent-implementation-and-impact

Ofsted (2022), 'Research review series: English.' *Ofsted*, https://www.gov.uk/government/publications/curriculum-research-review-series-english/curriculum-research-review-series-english

Ofsted (2024), 'Telling the story: the English education subject report'. *Ofsted*, https://www.gov.uk/government/publications/subject-report-series-english/telling-the-story-the-english-education-subject-report

Oracy Cambridge (2019), 'The Oracy Skills Framework and Glossary'. *Oracy Cambridge*, https://oracycambridge.org/wp-content/uploads/2020/06/The-Oracy-Skills-Framework-and-Glossary.pdf

Oracy Education Commission (2024), 'We need to talk'. *Oracy Education Commission*, https://oracyeducationcommission.co.uk/wp-content/uploads/2024/10/Future-of-Oracy-v23-web-13.pdf

Pashler, H., Bain, P., Bottge, B., Graesser, A., Koedinger, K., McDaniel, M. & Metcalfe, J. (2007), *Organizing Instruction and Study to Improve Student Learning*. Washington, DC: US Department of Education.

Perfetti, C., & Verhoeven, L. (2011), 'Morphological processing in reading acquisition: a cross linguistic perspective'. *Applied Psycholinguistics*, 32(03), 457–466.

Quigley, A. (2018), *Closing the Vocabulary Gap*. Abingdon: Routledge.

Quigley, A. (2020), *Closing the Reading Gap*. Abingdon: Routledge.

Quigley, A. (2022), 'Why even flawed research matters in education'. *TES magazine*, https://www.tes.com/magazine/teaching-learning/general/flawed-education-research-word-gap-language-development-hart-risley

Rasinski, T. (2006), 'Reading fluency instruction: Moving beyond accuracy, automaticity, and prosody'. *The Reading Teacher*, 59(7), 704–706.

Raskinski, T. V., Rupley, W. H., Paige, D. D., & Nichols, W. D. (2016), 'Alternative text types to improve reading fluency for competent to struggling readers'. *International Journal of Instruction*, 9(1), 163–178.

Ray, K., Dally, K., Rowlandson, L., Long Tam, K., & Lane, A. E. (2021), 'The relationship of handwriting ability and literacy in kindergarten: a systematic review'. *Reading and Writing*, 35, 1119–1155.

Recht, D. R., & Leslie, L. (1988), 'Effect of prior knowledge on good and poor readers' memory of text'. *Journal of Educational Psychology*, 80(1), 16–20.

Robbins, A. (2021), *Middle Leadership Mastery: A toolkit for subject and pastoral leaders*. Carmarthen: Crown House Publishing.

Robinson, A. (2007), *The story of writing*. London: Thames and Hudson.

Robinson, V. (2009), 'Open to learning conversations: Background paper introducing open to learning conversations' in Robinson, V. M., Hohepa, M. & Lloyd, C. *School leadership and student outcomes: Identifying what works and why – Iterative Best Evidence Synthesis Programme*. Wellington: New Zealand Ministry of Education.

Robinson, V. (2011), *Student-Centered Leadership*. San Francisco: Jossey-Bass.

Robinson, V. (2013), 'Leadership where it counts: making a bigger difference to your students'. *Teaching Times*, https://www.teachingtimes.com/leadership-where-it-counts/

Robinson, V. (2018), *Reduce Change to Increase Improvement*. Thousand Oaks, CA: Corwin.

Rosenshine, B. (2012), 'The principles of instruction research-based strategies that all teachers should know'. *American Educator*, 36(1), 12–39.

Sabatini, J., Wang, Z., & O'Reilly, T. (2019), 'Relating reading comprehension to oral reading performance in the NAEP fourth-grade special study of oral reading'. *Reading Research Quarterly*, 54(2), 253–271.

Saddler, B. (2012), *Teacher's Guide to Effective Sentence Writing*. New York: The Guilford Press.

Santangelo, T., & Graham, S. (2016), 'A Comprehensive Meta-analysis of Handwriting Instruction'. *Educational Psychology Review*, 28(2), 225–265.

Scarborough, H. S. (2001), 'Connecting early language and literacy to later reading (dis)abilities: Evidence, theory, and practice' in Neuman, S. & Dickinson, D. (eds) *Handbook for research in early literacy*. New York, NY: Guildford Press, pp. 97–110.

Scott, K. (2017), *Radical Candour: How to get what you want by saying what you mean*. London: Macmillan.

Seidenberg, M. (2017), *Language at the speed of sight: How we read, why so many can't and what can be done about it*. New York: Basic Books.

Seidenberg, M. (2020), 'Some context on context'. *Seidenberg Reading* https://seidenbergreading.net/2020/09/10/some-context-on-context/

Shanahan, T. (2017), 'How to Teach Fluency So That It Takes'. *Shanahanonliteracy. com*, https://www.shanahanonliteracy.com/blog/how-to-teach-fluency-so-that-it-takes

Sharples, J. Eaton, J. and Boughelaf, J. (2024), *A School's Guide to Implementation*. London: Education Endowment Foundation.

Shanahan, T. (2018), 'Is there really a 30 million-word gap?' *Shanahanonliteracy. com*, https://www.shanahanonliteracy.com/blog/is-there-really-a-30-million-word-gap

Share, D. (1995), 'Phonological recoding and self-teaching: Sine qua non of reading acquisition'. *Cognition*, 151–218.

Shearing, H. (2023), 'SATs: KS2 Year 6 reading paper revealed after row over difficulty'. *BBC News*, https://www.bbc.co.uk/news/education-65624697

Snowling, M. J., & Hulme, C. E. (2005), *The Science of Reading: A handbook*. Oxford: Blackwell Publishing.

Stahl, S., & Kuhn, M. (2002),' Making It Sound Like Language: Developing Fluency'. *Reading Teacher*, 55.

Stanovich, K. E., & Cunningham, A. E. (1993), 'Where does knowledge come from? Specific associations between print exposure and information acquisition'. *Journal of Educational Psychology*, 85(2), 211–229.

Stockard, J., Wood, T. W., Coughlin, C., & Khoury, C. R. (2018), 'The effectiveness of Direct Instruction curricula: a meta-analysis of a half century of research'. *Review of Educational Research*, 88(4), 479–507.

Such, C. (2021), *The Art and Science of Teaching Primary Reading*. London: Corwin.

Such, C. (2025), *Primary Reading Simplified*. London: Corwin.

Sweller, J. (1988), 'Cognitive load during problem solving: effects on learning'. *Cognitive Science*, 12, 257–285.

Terevainen-Goff, A., Flynn, M., Riad, L., Cole, A., & Clark, C. (2022), *Seldom-heard voices: Adult literacy in the UK*. London: National Literacy Trust.

The Open University (2024), 'Reading for Pleasure'. https://ourfp.org/

The Reading Ape (n.d.), 'Theoretical models of reading - better informed but none the wiser?' The *Reading Ape*, https://www.thereadingape.com/single-post/theoretical-models-of-reading-better-informed-but-none-the-wiser

The Reading Ape (n.d.), 'Hyperlexia: a deficit or a super-ability?' *The Reading Ape*, https://www.thereadingape.com/single-post/hyperlexia-a-deficit-or-a-super-ability

The Reading Ape (n.d.), 'English spelling! Do I really have to teach it?' *The Reading Ape*, https://www.thereadingape.com/single-post/english-spelling-do-i-really-have-to-teach-it

Turner, S. (2016), *Secondary Curriculum and Assessment Design*. London: Bloomsbury.

Van Geel, M., Visscher, A. J., & Teunis, B. (2017), 'School Characteristics Influencing the Implementation of a Data-Based Decision Making Intervention'. *School Effectiveness and School Improvement*, 28(3), pp. 443–462.

Weinstein, Y., Sumeracki, M., & Caviglioli, O. (2019), *Understanding How We Learn*. Abingdon: Routledge.

Wigfield, A., & Eccles, J. (eds) (2002), *Development of Achievement Motivation*. Cambridge, MA: Academic Press.

Wiliam, D., & Black, P. (1996), 'Meanings and Consequences: A basis for distinguishing formative and summative functions of assessment?' *British Educational Research Journal*, 22(5), 3570548.

Wiliam, D. (2018), *Creating The Schools Our Children Need: why what we're doing now won't help much (and what we can do instead)*. West Palm Beach: Learning Sciences.

Willingham, D. T. (2002), 'Ask the Cognitive Scientist: Inflexible Knowledge: The First Step to Expertise'. *American Educator*, https://www.aft.org/ae/winter2002/willingham

Willingham, D. (2017), *The Reading Mind: A Cognitive Approach to Understanding How the Mind Reads*. San Francisco, CA: Jossey-Bass.

Willingham, D. T. (2021), *Why Don't Students Like School?: A Cognitive Scientist Answers Questions About How the Mind Works and What It Means for the Classroom*. San Francisco, CA: Jossey-Bass.

Wolf, G. M. (2018), 'Developing reading automaticity and fluency: Revisiting what reading teachers know, putting confirmed research into current practice'. *Creative Education*, 9(6), 838.

Wolf, M. (2008), *Proust and the Squid: The Story and Science of the Reading Brain*. London: Icon Books.

Wolf, M., & Katzir-Cohen, T. (2001), 'Reading fluency and its intervention'. *Scientific Studies of Reading*, 5(3), 211–239.

Wold, M. (2018), *Reader, Come Home: The Reading Brain in a Digital World*. London: HarperCollins.

Young, R., Rose, R., & Nelson, R. (2015), 'Teaching Fluent Handwriting Remediates Many Reading-Related Learning Disabilities'. *Creative Education*, 6, 1752–1759.

Index

action plan proforma 214–16
administration 6
alphabetic principle 74
assessment 193
   of components within composites 60
   decoupling formative and
      summative 59–60
   domain, curricula and the sample
      for 56, 58
   fluency 68
   formative *see* formative assessment
   gathering feedback 62–3
   hinge questions, use of 62
   marker and circumstances 58
   PD session on responsive
      teaching 69–70
   phonics 67–8
   responsive teaching 61–2
   standardised benchmarking 67
   standardised comprehension 68
   summative *see* summative assessment
   understanding 55–6
   validity and reliability 57
Assessment for Learning (AfL) 58–9

behaviour 6
beyond early reading
   creating positive reading
      culture 109–10
   reading fluency 106–9
   reading for pleasure 106
   Reading Rope model, revisiting *see*
      Reading Rope model
   reading to learn phase 93
   vocabulary knowledge and
      background knowledge strands
      94, 95–6
blogs 19
BlueSky 18

change implementation
   'Deliver' phase 211–13
   'Explore' phase 206–9
   'Prepare' phase 209–11
   'Sustain' phase 213–14
Chartered College of Teaching, The 16
circumstances, and assessment 58
classroom talk, forms of 174–5
close-reading, lessons 104
code knowledge 78–80, 86, 89
cognitive demands management 21
cognitive load theory 19–21, 95–6
cognitive overload 20
cognitive science learning 19–20
   building pupil's background
      knowledge 21–4
   implications in classroom 20–1
collaborative curriculum reviews 185–6,
      199–201
component knowledge 30–2
composites, components before 30–1
contexts, comparing 14
cultural literacy, to support situation
      models 99
cumulative talk 174
curricular expertise 9–10
curriculum design and planning
      37–8
   hierarchical curriculum and learning
      over time 41–2
   knowledge categories to English
      38–41
   organising areas of 43–4
   phonics as curriculum content 42–3
   in school, with mixed-age classes 51–2
   teachers' understand 53
   texts selection 44–6
curriculum-related expectations
      approach 66–7

debating skills teaching 177–80
declarative knowledge 38
Development Matters 8
dialogic teaching 174
Direct Instruction (DI) programme 120
disciplinary knowledge 40, 41
discussion and debate 193
disputational talk 174
dyslexia 86–7

early reading teaching 73
   and beyond *see* beyond early reading
   building vocabulary 83–6
   code knowledge and phonics
      lesson 78–80
   fluency practice 78, 81–2
   language and listening
      comprehension 76–7
   PD session on whole-class
      fluency 91–2
   phonics screening check (PSC) 88–9
   phonics teaching for struggling
      readers 86–8
   Reading Rope model 77–8
   Simple View of Reading model 75–6
educational fallacies 15
Education Endowment Foundation (EEF)
   8, 15–16, 205–14
'Engaging with evidence guide' (Institute
   for Effective Education) 15
English Association, The 17
English Hubs 17
English-specific resources 16, 17
etymology 155–7, 161
Evidence Based Education Podcast
   18
evidence-informed decisions, approaches
   for 13–15
evidence-informed writing
   curriculum 132–4
evidence summaries and reviews 8
existing knowledge 21
explicit vocabulary instruction 83
exploratory talk 174–5
Expressive Writing 120

feedback gathering 62–3
fluency 81
   assessment 68
   fostering 21
   practice 78, 81–2
   reading fluency 78, 81–2, 106–
      9, 215–16
   whole-class, PD session on 91–2
formative assessment
   decoupling 59–60
   recording results of 63
   and responsive teaching 61–2
framework for English lesson 192–4
frequent recall 20

grammar-focused programmes 120

handwriting
   developmental stages of 145
   fluency 140
   instruction 140
   joined letters 143–4
   PD session on developing 146–7
   pre-writing skills for 141–2
   printed script teaching 142–3
   schemes' approaches 144
   skills 146–7
hierarchical curriculum 41–2
hinge questions 62
hyperlexia 107

impact, in curriculum planning 38
implementation
   action plan proforma 214–16
   in curriculum planning 37–8
   EEF guide to 205–14
   plans for success 203–5
implicit vocabulary instruction 83, 101
independent reading 104–5
inference skills 96
instruction 140
intent, in curriculum planning 37

keep-up intervention 80
knowledge 86

and background knowledge strands 94, 95–6
categories, to English 38–40, 41
sequencing 41–4

language comprehension 76
large-scale studies, prioritising 14
leaders 3–4
learning 20
lesson drop-ins 188–91
listening comprehension 76–7
literacy knowledge 99–100
long-term memory 20

marker 58
Mind the Gap 18
misspellings 151
modelling 130–1
model texts 130–1
morphology 153–5

National Association of Teachers of English, The 17
National Literacy Trust, The 17
National Professional Qualification (NPQ) 8, 9
non-declarative knowledge 39

Ofsted 187–8
optimising load 20
oracy 163–4
  approaches to teaching 165–6
  classroom talk, forms of 174–5
  components of 31–2
  debating skills teaching 177–80
  developing effective 164
  and dialogic teaching 174
  granular steps in oracy curriculum 169–73
  paired talk teaching 175–6
  PD session on building progression in oracy curriculum 181–2
  vocabulary importance in 167–9
oracy curriculum
  building progression into 181–2
  granular steps in 169–73
  importance in 167–9
Oracy Skills Framework 165–6

paired talk 175–6
participants, consistency of 14
PD session
  building knowledge with Reading Rope 111–12
  building progression into the oracy curriculum 181–2
  on co-creating a writing curriculum 136–7
  on collaborative curriculum review 199–201
  developing handwriting skills 146–7
  on responsive teaching 69–70
  using etymology in spelling lessons 161
  on whole-class fluency 91–2
phonic knowledge 42–3, 149–51
phonics assessment 67–8
phonics lesson 79
phonics screening check (PSC) 88–9
phonological processing difficulties 86–7
podcasts 18
polysyllabic words 152
positive QA culture 184–5
positive reading culture 109–10
practice, significance of 30
presentational talk 174–5
pre-teaching 192
pre-writing skills 141–2
primary education sources and guidance 15–19
primary English leader
  building cultural literacy to support situation models 99
  creating implementation plans 205
  creating model texts 131
  curriculum design ideas for 52
  evidence-informed decisions, approaches for 13–15
  improving subject knowledge on handwriting development 145

Index

role of 3–4
printed script teaching 142–3
procedural knowledge 39
professional development 5, 53
progression in English
   building understanding 32–3
   components of oracy 31–2
   deep knowledge of similes, developing 33–4
   growing component knowledge 30–1
   progression maps and outcomes 29–30
   reading and writing texts 34–5
pupil's background knowledge 21–2

quality assurance (QA)
   creating positive culture of 184–5
   for curriculum planning and resourcing 185–7
   of English teaching and learning 187–8
   framework for English lesson 192–4
   lesson drop-ins, performing productive 188–91
   PD session on collaborative curriculum review 199–201
   pitfalls of 183–4
   in pupil work and outcomes 194–7
   responding to initial inferences 197–8

reading 193
   fluency 78, 81–2, 106–9, 215–16
   and text discussion 105–6
   and writing 67–8
Reading Ape, The 19
reading-lesson sequence 102–6
Reading Rope model
   in beyond early reading 93–5
   building knowledge with 111–12
   building vocabulary 101
   to develop inference skills 96
   in early reading teaching 77–8
   for reading-lesson sequence 102–6
   and situation models 96–8
ResearchED 17
research evidence

Chartered College of Teaching 16
cognitive science learning 19–20
Education Endowment Foundation (EEF) 15–16
English-specific resources 16, 17
guiding principles for 13–15
social media platforms 18–19
research results, trusting 14
Research Review Series: English 8
responsive teaching 61–2, 69–70
retrieval practice 20, 192

sampling pupils' knowledge 58
schemas 20
schemes' approaches 144
school culture 5
school improvement 6
school leadership, problems of 4, 5–7
Science of Reading: the Podcast 18
self 7
sentence-level writing 120–3
sentences
   cohesion across 24
   knowledge of 23
Shanahan on Literacy 19
similes, developing deep knowledge of 33–4
Simple View of Reading model 75–6
simplification 14
situation models 96–8
skills, and knowledge 41
social media platforms 18
sound-spelling correspondences, teaching 159–60
sound swap games 81
spaced practice for phonics units 150–1
spaced retrieval 20
spelling teaching
   PD session using etymology in 161
   planning for common errors in 157–9
   sound–spelling correspondences, teaching 159–60
   syllabic approach 152
   through morphology 153–5
   through phonic knowledge 149–51

using etymology 155–7
ways for 151–2
spoken words, mismatching with 75
statutory and non-statutory guidance 8
subject knowledge on handwriting development 145
substantive knowledge 40, 41
summative assessment 64–5
   approaches to 65–6
   curriculum-related expectations 66–7
   decoupling 59–60
   of reading 67–8
   standardised benchmarking assessments 67
   teacher assessment 65–6
   of writing 68
support levels 21
syllabic practice 152

targeted planning 21
Teach Meets 9
Telling the story 8
texts selection 44–50
Thinking Deeply About Primary Education 18
3Rs, The 19

UK Literacy Association, The 17
understanding, building of 32–3

vocabulary 192
   attainment stage 168
   building 83–6, 101
   development 21–2
   importance in oracy curriculum 167–9
   knowledge 86, 95–6
   teaching 83–6, 101
   tiers 83–4

whole-class fluency 91–2
working memory 20, 96
writers, developing 116–17
writing
   complexity of 116
   content for 124–5
   curriculum for 117–23
   developing writers 116–17
   evidence-informed writing curriculum 132–4
   grammar-focused programmes, research on 120
   grammar teaching and punctuation 119–20, 122–3
   history of 73–4
   long-term planning and teaching sequences for 125–9
   mismatching with spoken words 75
   model texts and modelling for, providing 130–1
   PD session on co-creating a writing curriculum 136–7
   sentence-level writing 120–3
   spelling 118–19
writing curriculum, co-creating 136–7

X (formerly Twitter) 18